500ml

450ml

400ml

350ml

THE **PRESENTATION LAB**

500ml

450ml

400ml

350ml

THE **PRESENTATION LAB**

Learn the Formula
Behind Powerful
Presentations

PL

ISBN 978-1-118-68700-0
53000

9 781118 687000

S I M O N   M O R T O N

011001010111010010110010110100101
010110010100010111001101100101010110
011001010111010010110010110100101

WILEY

For Lisa, Beth, and Peter—you make me brave. x

This book is the culmination of almost a decade of thinking, sleeping, reading, crafting, and doing presentations. This occasionally unhealthy obsession wouldn't be possible without the friendship and support of the amazing people that make up the Eyeful Presentations team across the world. In particular, my hat is doffed and my gratitude overflows (in chronological order) to Dan, Sal, Faz, and Zo—you're very special people. Thanks for the support (I'm still wearing it).

Thank you also to the amazing customers who have chosen to join us on the journey thus far. Your faith, enthusiasm, and willingness to challenge the status quo is the key to great presentations. I'm glad we've been able to repay your trust over the years.

Finally, a huge thank you to the hyper-talented Alex and Phil for the incredible designs that make this book all the more special. Thank you also for admirably resisting the temptation to strangle me whenever I popped into the studio with yet another idea or scrappy drawing.

Thanks and Acknowledgments

Simon Morton

Element A
Introduction

Element B
The Basic Tools for the Job

Element C
The Base Elements of Your Presentation

A₁ 004	**B₁** 030	
Before We Get Started…The Presentation Labs Hypothesis	The Power of Inspiration: From Okay…to Good…to Optimized	

A₁ 004
Before We Get Started…The Presentation Labs Hypothesis

B₁ 030
The Power of Inspiration: From Okay…to Good…to Optimized

A₂ 008
Welcome to the Presentation Lab

B₂ 034
The Appliance of Science: A Beginner's Guide

A₃ 012
What This Book Is *Not* About…

B₃ 038
Business Storytelling: What's All the Fuss About?

C₃ 058
Audiences: The Most Complex of Beasts…

C₆ 086
Messaging: Simplicity Is Not Stupidity

A₄ 016
The Impact (& Source) of Poor Presentations

B₄ 042
Business Storytelling: Getting Your Story Straight

C₁ 054
The Base Elements of Your Presentation

C₄ 074
The Audience Pathway

C₇ 088
Give Them Something They Will Remember… And Then Let It Travel

A₅ 020
Myth Busting

B₅ 048
Introducing Presentation Optimization

C₂ 056
Respect the Audience

C₅ 082
Message: What's the Point?

C₈ 092
Structuring Your Message: The Power of the Storyflow

The Presentation Lab
Table of Contents

The Presentation Lab is an exciting and dynamic place, with explosive creativity everywhere you look. As the lab assistant I'll be guiding you safely through, while making sure you don't miss key elements.

PL

Foreword

The least important thing about a presentation is the presentation itself.

The most important thing is the effect it has on your audience—that is, what your audience does and feels as a result of hearing you speak.

Your presentation is a means to an end, not the end itself.

But people don't view it like that. Instead, they tend to prepare by thinking:

What do I want to say?

What slides have I got that I can reuse?

Who can I delegate the prep to?

Unsurprisingly, this often leads to overlong, uninspiring, one-way rants that do more harm than good. I'm sure you've heard a few of these in the past week alone. And, let's face it, we all hate sitting through them, don't we?

Now, at last, here's a book that can change all that.

I first met Simon a few years ago. To be honest, I was a little wary beforehand. I'd met lots of "PowerPoint experts" before. I'd found most wore "to a man with a hammer, everything looks like a nail" blinkers. You know the type of thing: "You're delivering a presentation? Great—we design slides. Let's discuss how we can make yours whizzy and shiny."

But he was the complete opposite.

Like me, Simon's core belief is that a presentation is an audience thing. They—not the presenter—decide whether the presentation is good or not.

It's they who decide whether to follow the Call To Action. So it's they who should be our sole focus throughout. Get this right, and everyone benefits. It makes things easy and quick. It's more pleasant. Things get done.

This book will help you deliver the best presentations of your life. You'll learn techniques that will permanently change the way you speak to others. I know this, because I've seen it happen. Simon's company and I have worked together many times, helping thousands of people—both presenters and audiences—enjoy presentations more and transforming the way companies communicate, leaders lead, and sales teams sell.

This book will show you how to take your audiences with you on a journey, in such a way that they want to—and do—the things you want.

Better still, it will change how you feel about presentations. Because, let's face it, what you say on the outside mirrors what you're thinking on the inside.

But best of all? Your audiences will love that you've read it.

And when that happens, everybody wins.

Andy Bounds

Communication expert and author of international best sellers *The Snowball Effect* and *The Jelly Effect*

THE PRESENTATION LAB

Introduction

Element **A** B C D E F G H

A

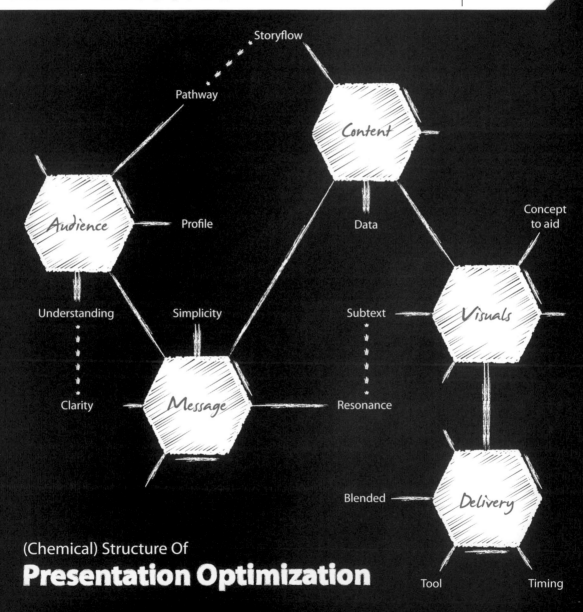

Storyflow

Pathway

Content

Audience

Profile

Data

Concept to aid

Understanding

Simplicity

Subtext

Visuals

Clarity

Message

Resonance

Blended

Delivery

Tool

Timing

(Chemical) Structure Of
Presentation Optimization

Clear communication has never been as important in business as it is today. The examples range from something as simple as crafting a lucid e-mail to a colleague, all the way to sharing a vision and inciting passion in an audience via a more complex presentation. The ability to do these things—and so many others—is a must-have for every successful businessperson today.

The exciting news is that communication—business and otherwise—has changed beyond all recognition over the past few years.

So much of our professional interaction has moved away from the "old school," formal scenario of standing and presenting to a group of businesspeople (often in a horseshoe configuration of desks . . . just to make you feel that little more nervous/inferior).

Nowadays, we tend to find ourselves communicating quite informally—in person over a coffee/beer in an airport lounge or at networking events and online via social media or webinars. More often than not, the opportunity for our communication (and presentations) to be interactive crops up, and we should be grabbing these chances with both hands.

Wherever you happen be when these exchanges begin, you have a chance to not simply shine as a presenter but, more important, to share your ideas, vision, proposition, or just plain old story in a powerful way. Add to that the fast-growing list of presentation tools and technologies now available to us and we're in a golden age of presentation development. Happy days.

Of course, some people seem to have that innate ability to get up there and present . . . and others don't. We all have those wonderfully talented colleagues who are usually so gregarious—but who freeze as soon as they step up to the front of an audience (heck, you might be one of them!). There are also those incredibly bright individuals who have so much to share that they end up confusing their audience rather than imparting their knowledge.

Sadly, people's inability to clearly communicate their message through presentations in all its forms (and we're not just talking about PowerPoint here, as you'll find out later) can have a devastating impact on what should be a brilliant career.

One of the reasons there are so many presentation-coaching companies out there (most are, strangely enough, run by ex-actors who know little or nothing about business) is that these frustrated but brilliant colleagues recognize the importance of getting this part of their job right. And sometimes, this coaching works, because it was their **soft** skills that needed a spit and polish. But too often, the issue lies much deeper—in the creation and development of the entire presentation process. Business presentations should not be seen as a grand performance; they should be seen as a powerful interaction between presenter and audience. And it's the latter that this book focuses on.

There are endless books, coaching companies, and websites that offer hints and tips on managing the soft skills part of the process (you know the kind of thing—don't jingle change in your pocket, don't stand in front of the projector, check your zipper before you go on stage). However, there's a very scant offering in terms of constructing and visually telling your story.

The Presentation Lab is here to change that . . . for good. Over the next eight sections, I'm going to share with you the steps and stages required to create a presentation story that not only works for you as the presenter but, more important, delivers exactly what your **audience** needs—no matter what environment you're presenting in or what demographic/ethnic/socioeconomic mix your audience is.

You see, the audience is the most important factor in the presentation process.

And keeping them at the core of everything we do is vital to the success of the presentation. But, we're already getting ahead of ourselves. First, let's look at where the concept of the Presentation Lab came from in the first place.

A person can have the **greatest idea** in the world—completely different and novel—but if that person can't convince enough people, it doesn't matter.

Gregory Berns, Neuroscientist

Th e idea for a "Presentation Lab" has been bubbling away for some time within my business, Eyeful Presentations.

We wanted a place to test new ideas, invite customers and friends to try different approaches out, and never have to worry that they were making themselves look daft in front of a live audience. And the Presentation Lab does just that. We give people the opportunity to use new technologies, develop innovative hooks and story structures, and generally get completely immersed.

More exciting is the fact that by creating a truly immersive environment, we are able to equip the most engaged, influential people within a business with the skills and vision to make a real difference to their corporate view of presentations. The people who visit our Eyeful Labs facility in the United Kingdom—or, I would imagine, who've spent their hard-earned money on this book—are the same people who *make change happen* within an organization. Companies need only a handful of passionate and committed voices to point out the futility of poor presentation thinking, and build sufficient momentum for change.

Business presentations need to change—of that there is no doubt. The theory and approach we embrace at the Presentation Lab will equip you with the insight, tools, and passion to affect that change within your own organization.

The first step in getting your head around the Presentation Lab method is to recognize the reality that there is no silver bullet that addresses all of your organization's presentation woes.

You come to the answer by using a variety of different options and solutions, mixing them up and testing them in as open and engaging way as you can. And hopefully, your company can become a bit like the Presentation Lab in some small way—a fun place where sometimes the most random aside can spark new ideas and presentation inspiration.

The Presentation Lab

PL

Warning

Creativity at work

I remember working with the UK executive team of a large information technology (IT) company a few years ago. They were up against quite a challenge, following a tough couple of years in a crowded marketplace. They'd come to us to support them in the launch of a new Cloud-based service. The understandably anxious Sales and Marketing Director wanted to push the Cloud message's flexibility, believing it would give them early-mover advantage. Unfortunately, the company's CEO saw nothing other than a return on investment (ROI) message working as a way to get them out of the mire. After a couple of hours facilitating a lively but increasingly fractious discussion over the merits of each message, we broke for coffee and a chance to chat about something *other* than work.

Being both a keen gardener and British, the topic of the weather quickly came up (it's a cliché but true!). I mentioned that my Spring crop of vegetables was suffering due to the perpetually overcast days we'd experienced for the past few weeks.

"You see, clouds don't always make for good news," I muttered, still worrying about my green tomatoes.

"Um . . . that's it . . . !" sparked up the CEO.

What followed was an incredibly speedy and gratifying turnaround in presentation message. All parties threw themselves into it with true gusto; there was a real sense of shared passion and vision in where we were heading with the message. Out went the somewhat waffly focus on the technology being "cool and sexy," as did the well-trodden ROI message. Instead, both were replaced by a beautifully simple message that played directly to their audience's anxieties: We can tell you—in one-syllable words—whether your business could benefit from the new Cloud technology in terms of efficiency, technology costs, and flexibility, and if it can't, we'll tell you why not—and the other options available to you.

That pretty much sums up the Presentation Lab approach. We want to create an environment where new ideas can spark relatively random thoughts and comments and then inject them with sufficient passion and enthusiasm to see them cross over the line from great idea to reality. It's about giving you the skills and, equally important, the confidence to do this within your own organization. It will be fun, challenging and, on occasion, headache inducing, but I assure you it will be worthwhile . . .

Shall we begin?

The Presentation Lab Methodology

Take one disillusioned presenter

Immerse in creative environment

Wait for ideas to come to the surface

Inject with high levels of passion and enthusiasm

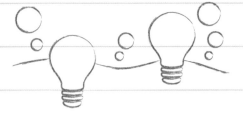

Take away presentation perfection

THE PRESENTATION LAB

What This Book Is *Not* About . . .

A₃

Element **A** B C D E F G H

Wr iting a book is one of the most exciting things I've ever done. It's my chance to put down in black and white (or whichever color scheme the boys in the studio agree upon) the thoughts, frustrations, and lessons learned over many years of working with huge companies to improve the impact of their presentations and their engagement with audiences.

It's like a musician laying down their first album after many years of touring and playing in front of live audiences. There's just so much to share. And that's where it can get tricky.

If I try to squeeze everything I know into one book, it'll be a mess. We're bound to fail if I overdo it and attempt to cure all the presentation ills that befall businesses every day. As you'll come to learn in later chapters, it's as much about what you leave out as what you keep and deliver on.

So with this in mind, here's a list of the things we won't be covering here, along with the reasons why:

NOT IN THE PRESENTATION LAB

Soft Skills

We have some truly gifted soft skills trainers within my business who are located all over the globe. They spend their (very long) days working with presenters to improve their ability to take the story we have created for them and knock it out of the park in terms of personal performance. They have an extraordinary impact; I've witnessed previously timid executives morph into powerful orators—and, if I'm being frank, I've seen many arrogant and overly confident speakers tweaked and coerced into becoming more genuine and selfless presenters. It's powerful stuff.

The reason I'm not including any of the soft skills alchemy in this book is that in my experience, developing and enhancing your presentation soft skills chops is an incredibly personal journey. Our trainers understand that many of the individual foibles that keep people from delivering a presentation with passion, gusto, and commitment involve more than learning where to stand, how to project your voice, and what to do with your hands. At its best, it's a process that's tailored to each presenter. Therefore, squeezing a chapter in about this very involved and important element of presenter success (note: not **presentation** success . . . we'll be sure to sort that out for you) seemed a little silly—and not the best use of our (or your) time.

Getting to Prettier PowerPoint

As we'll demonstrate over the course of this book, we love PowerPoint. We think it's a tremendous tool—when *used properly* and in *appropriate situations*. We also recognize that, despite the somewhat boring and unoriginal bad press around its use, it's still a firm favorite among the vast majority of business presenters.

In a similar vein to the soft skills stuff, a good PowerPoint slide is a bespoke creation. And we *will* be explaining how to create visuals to accompany your story. They will need to fit into the flow of the presentation; sit nicely alongside you, the presenter, as a natural extension of your message and style; and help drive your communication home.

What we *won't* be covering is click-by-click use, demonstrating how to work with templates, create impactful animations, or insert videos. There are a plethora of books available for these elements depending on the version of PowerPoint (or Keynote for that matter) you're using, and frankly I think we have more important issues to cover, such as messaging, story structure, and audience engagement. Don't you?

How the Presentation Industry Has Got It All Wrong

A strong statement, I know, but ever more apparent as I consider the way business communication is evolving these days. People are presenting in different environments, using new technologies and absorbing information in new and exciting ways. Yet on the whole, the presentation sector has not reacted at all. If anything, it seems to be actively *resisting* the new reality.

Let me explain.

Everything about the presentation messaging and design sector is set up to address "traditional" presentation dilemmas. These sit firmly in the formal environment of giving a prepared, preplanned, presentation to an audience that typically does not ask questions along the way.

And this is a fine approach for many kinds of public appearances. Bid presentations fit this model rather nicely, as do conferences, seminars, and, to a certain extent, webinars.

But—countless other presentations situations have moved on from this.

Many of the best and most successful sales presentations are, at their core, *conversations*.

The ability to interact, respond, and engage with an audience is incredibly powerful—and incredibly difficult to do with many of the restrictive presentation structures and tools foisted upon sales teams the world over.

Much the same can be said for those fortuitous and serendipitous moments when you present informally, either on a napkin over a beer in an airport bar or using a whiteboard as part of an inspiring and free-flowing discussion.

Despite this important change in the presentation landscape, most experts in this field spend their time focusing on those diminishing formal situations. Designers work on linear PowerPoint decks to deliver visuals for the formal situation; authors write books about developing presentations to engage audiences in a formal situation—and ultimately, these are becoming increasingly irrelevant. Rather than worrying about coaching people on how to stand, pace themselves, and breathe for formal presentations, shouldn't organizations invest in having their teams *truly* understand their story—and be able to share it with passion, relevant content, and visuals that they can use in all kinds of different situations?

Organizations need to ask themselves a crucial question: Does my presentation work only as a formal PowerPoint? Or can I share it "on the back of an envelope" if the audience and situation demands it?

THE PRESENTATION LAB

The Impact (& Source) of Poor Presentations

A₄

There's no getting away from it: Business communication is in crisis. Boardrooms across the globe are grinding to a halt under the weight of poor presentations. Decisions are taking longer and, sadly, thanks to presentations' shockingly inadequate quality, people are often making these decisions based on incorrect assumptions and patchy, poorly presented data.

We cannot overstate the negative impact these substandard presentations have on business. Many moons ago (excuse the pun), NASA got pulled into a storm of debate about the inefficiency of PowerPoint when people began pointing to the presentation software the "source of all evil" and a contributing factor in the Columbia tragedy. It was argued that NASA had become overreliant on PowerPoint when it came to presenting and debating complex engineering issues.

NASA's Columbia Accident Investigation Board said in their report, "It is easy to understand how a senior manager might read this PowerPoint slide and not realize that it addresses a life-threatening situation."

Although one could debate long into the night about the part PowerPoint had to play, one very obvious, very important fact remains:

The people at NASA failed to communicate clearly.

The fact that they are incredibly intelligent, eloquent people really didn't matter—their presentation failed. Adding to that the fact that they chose, in retrospect, the wrong tool for the job is neither here nor there. They neglected to present their content in a way that communicated the message clearly, and the subsequent decision made around that board table resulted in the tragic death of seven brave men and women.

There's no denying the fact incidents such as NASA's wrong decision are happening in businesses across the globe every day. As you're reading this, someone somewhere is presenting information in such a verbose and complicated manner that the decision makers sitting before them (who, let's be frank, the presenter likely had to chase down with all of his energy to actually book the meeting in the first place) have mentally checked out. Their minds are on the stack of e-mails slowly building up back at their desks (or, if they're a little on the rude side, on the e-mails they're checking on their phones as the presenter sweats his way through yet another PowerPoint slide).

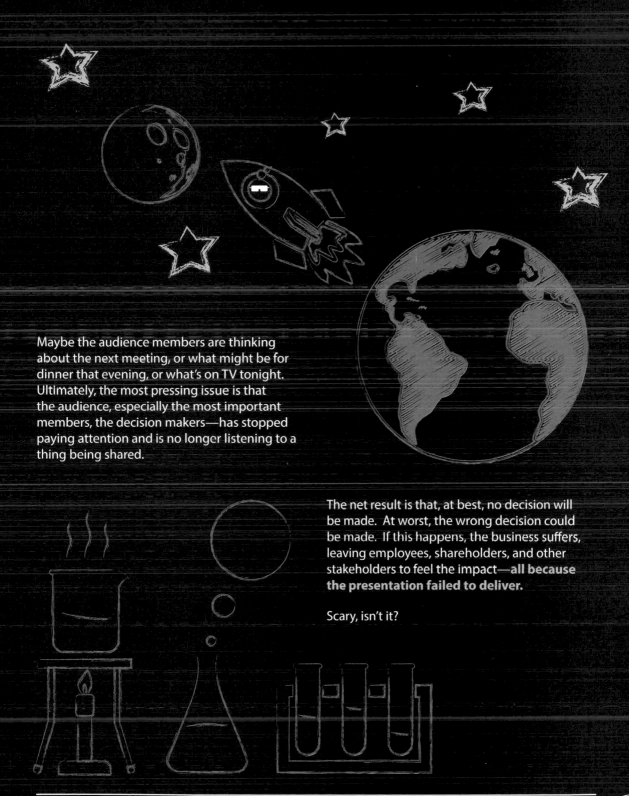

Maybe the audience members are thinking about the next meeting, or what might be for dinner that evening, or what's on TV tonight. Ultimately, the most pressing issue is that the audience, especially the most important members, the decision makers—has stopped paying attention and is no longer listening to a thing being shared.

The net result is that, at best, no decision will be made. At worst, the wrong decision could be made. If this happens, the business suffers, leaving employees, shareholders, and other stakeholders to feel the impact—**all because the presentation failed to deliver.**

Scary, isn't it?

So why do such a large number of presentations fail? There are a number of factors, ranging from time and skills through to executive support and recognition of the part presentations play in clear communication.

When working with sales and marketing teams, we will often highlight a behavior that we call the Presentation Paradox.

The Presentation Paradox is prevalent in companies large and small across the globe and manifests itself in a last-minute panic to prepare a presentation for a sales meeting.

Chances are the sales meeting will have been the culmination of vast amounts of work and investment in people, marketing, and skills training. If you ever want to see all the color drain from a CEO's face, have him or her calculate the true cost of getting a trained salesperson in front of a qualified prospect; the numbers are mind-boggling.

Yet it is only at the last minute that the thought of a presentation enters the salesperson's mind. The inevitable response is either copying and pasting some slides together (also known as a Frankenstein presentation), passing it on to a Personal Assistant to create, or working on it all night in front of the TV—all surefire ways of creating a mediocre presentation at best.

Despite these avoidable "crimes against presenting," PowerPoint is often the tool that gets blamed for the failings of the presenter! This injustice puts me in mind of some other myths that need busting . . .

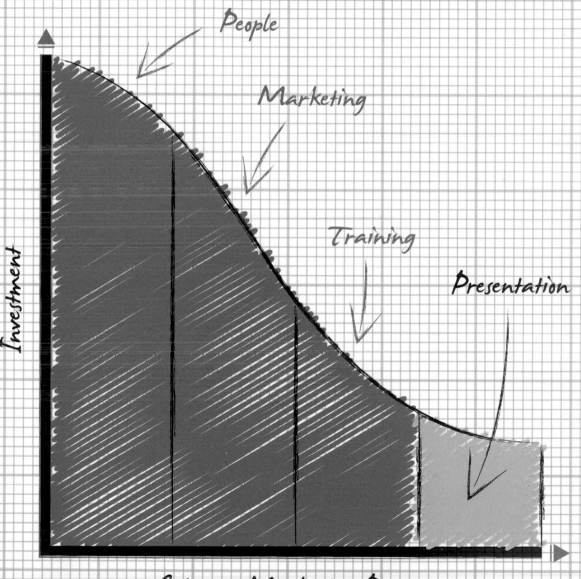

The Presentation Paradox

People

Marketing

Training

Presentation

Investment

Sales & Marketing Process

Myth Busting

A$_5$

Element   **A** B C D E F G H

One of my biggest frustrations (and I wager, one of the reasons for poor presentations becoming the norm in business today) is the prevalence of myths that surround presentations.

We've all been party to the alleged wise words from the "business sage"—and unfortunately over time, many of these opinions have become fact. Here are some of my favorites:

Myth #1: PowerPoint Is Intrinsically Evil

A couple of years ago, a Swiss chap by the name of Matthias Poehm came up with a cunning plan: He started a "Ban PowerPoint" political party. Poehm's movement garnered worldwide publicity (which coincided rather fortuitously with his book's launch) and got everyone with a blog back on the old hobbyhorse: PowerPoint should be banned by all for the crime of dumbing down business presentations.

PowerPoint's biggest failing is simply that it's too damned easy to use. Microsoft has made available to people all over the World—and businesspeople in particular—a tool that can help deliver powerful visual presentations. The drawback is that only a tiny percentage of these people have a clue as to how to *begin* to create such a presentation. Yet this (unfortunately) doesn't seem to deter them. The generally accepted best guesstimate is that 30 million* PowerPoint presentations are created or delivered every day, which goes to demonstrate the ease by which death by a thousand bullets can be achieved.

However, blaming PowerPoint's ease of use for poor communication within the business boardroom is like blaming Microsoft's Word program for bad speeches or Outlook for poor e-mail content.

The blame sits squarely with the person who sat in front of the computer and his or her inability to understand or learn the skills required to deliver a powerful visual presentation.

*Note: No one has been able to verify this number, but it seems like as good a guess as we're going to get based on the number of legal and bootleg copies of Microsoft Office that reside on personal computers (PCs) across the World.

Myth #2: The Slides Are the Presentation

The most revealing sign that the tail is wagging the dog is when a colleague—or even worse, a prospect—asks you to send the deck of slides while referring to them as "the presentation."

As will become clear through the pages of this book that a presentation is a combination of many things, the most important being the presenter. Sending a slide deck through to a prospect is akin to sending the visuals that comprise your website or brochure minus any copy. The visuals wouldn't (and *shouldn't!*) make sense without the accompanying commentary—which, surprise, surprise, comes from you, the presenter.

One of the most frustrating results of this sort of thinking is that people create slides that aim to serve two purposes: one as a visual prompt to support the presenter (the *right* way to think about PowerPoint) and the other as a "leave behind," which inevitably means slides full of explanatory text to make up for the absence of the presenter. The net result fails on both counts; presenters sacrifice visual impact for the inclusion of copy. But wary of having *too* much text on the slide (for we know this is a bad thing, right?), there is insufficient detail in the words.

The impact of this on the audience is obvious: When faced with the challenge of trying to work their way through text heavy slides while simultaneously listening to the presenter talking away, they do neither particularly well—and ultimately end up mentally checking out. The fancy scientific explanation of this phenomenon is Cognitive Load Theory, which, in layperson's terms, means that human beings are not particularly adept at doing more than one thing at a time. (Although this is not exactly groundbreaking news, it's handy to drop into a dinner party conversation should the need arise.)

In the world of presentations, compromise always comes at a cost. And the cost in this case is a confused, unengaged, and frustrated audience—which is clearly *not* what we're after.

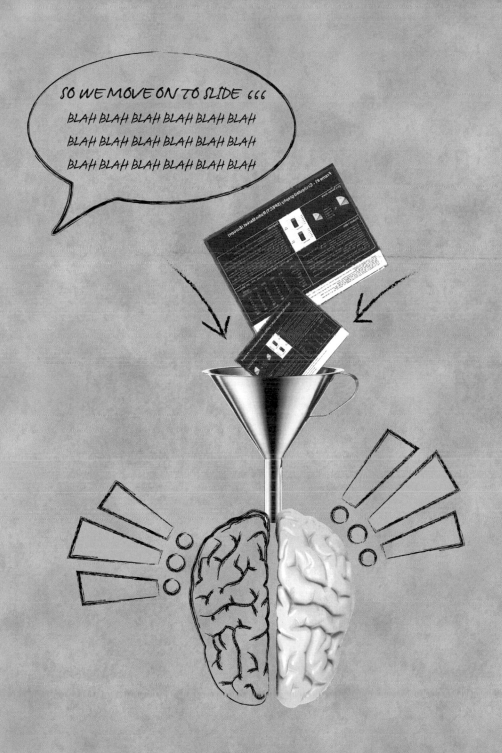

Myth #3: Presentation Zen/Typography

To mangle a well-used phrase, with great influence comes great responsibility. The well-respected Godfather of Presentation Design, Garr Reynolds, released his 2007 book, *Presentation Zen*, to international acclaim. At last, someone had created a reference book on slide design that neither condemned the use of PowerPoint nor alienated its audience with overly complex design-speak and waffle.

Well done, Garr.

There is no doubt that Garr Reynolds has made a difference to the way people think about their visuals. However, as is too often the case with this sort of book, far too many people have lost sight of his premise due to misinterpretation and skim reading.

It's easy to spot the warning signs that a presentation has been "Zen'd" without the presenter really understanding the finer details. The use of beautifully shot, high-resolution images that (although artistically gorgeous) add nothing to the story being told are surefire signals that someone has read only the liner notes and didn't really understand Garr's major points. Look out for close-up shots of nature, ripples in water, or, God forbid, pebbles stacked up on top of each other as examples of where the hunt for a great image on Corbis or iStockphoto has come at the cost of true visual communication.

Much the same can be said for a trend that we saw rear it's well-designed but ultimately ineffective head a few years ago when Wordle came out.

If you've not had a chance to Wordle, I highly recommend it. It's a lot of fun, takes no time, and provides you with a quick and artistically pleasing way of pulling together a lot of words onto a slide.

Here's a Wordle from our own blog:

Nice, eh? But here's the rub: Although it might look very nice, it's of little or no use to you as a presentation visual unless you really are looking to highlight the fact that *presentations* is a key term in your search engine criteria. It looks great printed out as a poster and wonderful as a blog visual, but it does little more than confuse a live presentation audience as they'll spend their time trying to read the fancy font and totally stop listening to you.

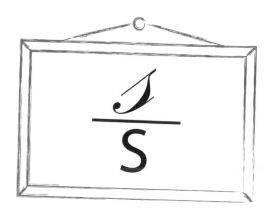

In short, style over substance never works.

Myth #4: The 10/20/30 Rule

This comes courtesy of Guy Kawasaki, a very clever man who has done wonders in his field of business. However, his thinking when it comes to presentations is dated, is incredibly restrictive, and relies on an assumption that all presentations come with a slide deck—which, as you'll learn later on, should no longer be a prerequisite.

Guy comes from a venture capital background, where time is money and patience runs short. As such, he and his brethren have little time for presentations that meander and fail to get to the point. That makes him like the rest of us: We don't want to take up our precious time with a presentation that doesn't hit the mark either. My issue with this 10/20/30 model is as follows:

Rule 1

No more than 10 slides are allowed, in a very particular order. Now, some elements of Guy's structure work well for me. I like the (seemingly obvious) idea of opening with the issue you are looking to address. Although there's nothing particularly revolutionary about this, it makes for a pleasant change to the "this is how big we are, this is a picture of our head office" introduction slide that befalls most below-par business presentations.

I do have one beef, though: Sticking religiously to 10 slides is simply too restrictive. Failure to give your message sufficient room to grow and develop is as detrimental to the audience as stuffing every slide with content and noise. Less is more is a good guide, but don't fall into the trap of hampering yourself.

Rule 2

Speak for no more than 20 minutes. Again, this is great advice for a pitch where you have been allocated a full 60 minutes. However, it's irrelevant (and potentially damaging) for other types of presentation formats. As we will explain in later sections, many presentations have moved on from the "I speak; you listen" format of old. A passionate and engaging conversation for much longer than 20 minutes is likely to be a sign of a productive presentation.

Rule 3

Font size of 30. This is spot on; if only PowerPoint and Keynote could force good practice like this with a button to override those who really like seeing their audience strain to read their slides. But this font size rule isn't sufficient. Making your text large enough to read is a great place to start, but if, in doing so, all you've done is increase the size of too much text. This doesn't address the bigger issue: presenters forgetting the importance of visualization as part of their presentation experience. If the only purpose of PowerPoint is to throw up large words, why not simply print them off and hand them over to your audience?

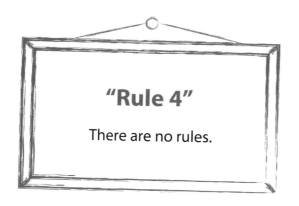

"Rule 4"

There are no rules.

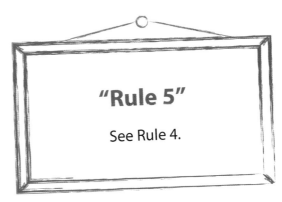

"Rule 5"

See Rule 4.

Guy provides some great presentation advice, but just as with Garr's teachings, people need to look beyond the basic "rules." The problem is that people have taken Guy's wise words about a very specific presentation environment—the venture capital pitch—out of context and applied them to *all* presentations. So we now have people delivering internal communications in the same frantic style as someone pitching for multimillion-dollar investment.

I guess the thing to take away from this grumpy section is not that these myths themselves are *bad*. In fact, the original ideas behind them all stack up and are designed to help us all develop better presentations. The issue is that the ideas have mutated; they have been twisted and tweaked to fit situations for which they were never designed and suffered at the hands of Chinese whispers or people who only read the *Cliff's Notes* version.

Alas, dear reader, there is no silver bullet for developing your presentations. (We know; we've looked.) As explained in the next section, success is about equipping yourself with the right tools, know-how, and most important, frame of mind to move your presentation from okay all the way to "Optimized."

THE PRESENTATION LAB

The Basic Tools
for the Job

B

Element   A **B** C D E F G H

No matter how many books you read, training events you sign up for (and hopefully, attend), or YouTube tutorials you watch, the simple fact is that there is nothing that makes a presentation work better than that flash of *inspiration*.

Without inspiration, you're merely playing around the edges, applying lipstick to a pig, or rearranging the deckchairs on the Titanic.

A presentation without inspiration is destined to fail.

The good news is the inspiration for your next presentation is everywhere. Look around you and you'll see hundreds, nay, *thousands*, of things that can act as the catalyst for a brilliant presentation.

Someone might make an off-the-cuff remark that gives you that all-important spark. You might read an article over someone's shoulder on the train into work that gets the creative juices flowing. It could be something as completely non business related as a TV show, a family photograph, or a joke or a song on the radio.

It doesn't matter *where* the inspiration for your presentation comes from; what's important is to know what to do with it once you get it.

The good news is that inspiration counts for a huge proportion of what makes for a good presentation. In my opinion—which is based on working with hundreds of companies on thousands of vitally important presentations— once you have the inspiration element in place, you're about 85 percent of the way there.

85%

15%

INSPIRATION   HARD WORK

PRESENTATION

INSPIRATION

THE PRESENTATION LAB

Inspired | I

The perhaps not-so-good news is that the remaining 15 percent is pretty damned hard work. I mean *really* hard. But it's also this last 15 percent that makes all the difference. It turns your idea from an average, run-of-the-mill, or even painful presentation (the ones we experience day in and day out) into something remarkable—an **optimized** presentation.

Just 15 percent makes all the difference—yet it doesn't rely on any expertise in PowerPoint, Keynote, or the plethora of other fancy presentation software packages.

Nor does it rely on you being the most effervescent speaker known to man. And the 15 percent doesn't require an armful of college, university, or marketing degrees.

Every business presenter out there can apply this magical 15 percent. You have the ingredients in place already, and if you don't, you can source them easily enough by juggling your schedule and reprioritizing a few things:

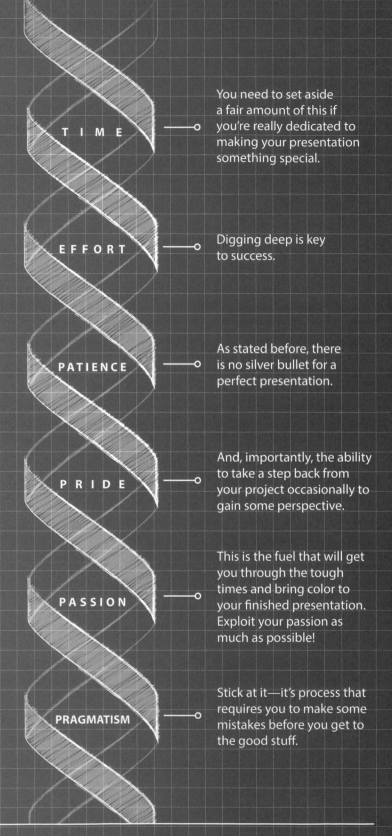

TIME
You need to set aside a fair amount of this if you're really dedicated to making your presentation something special.

EFFORT
Digging deep is key to success.

PATIENCE
As stated before, there is no silver bullet for a perfect presentation.

PRIDE
And, importantly, the ability to take a step back from your project occasionally to gain some perspective.

PASSION
This is the fuel that will get you through the tough times and bring color to your finished presentation. Exploit your passion as much as possible!

PRAGMATISM
Stick at it—it's process that requires you to make some mistakes before you get to the good stuff.

By applying the ideas and processes in this book, you'll move along the Presentation Optimization scale, culminating in a presentation that engages audiences in the most powerful way possible—prompting them to make changes and view things differently.

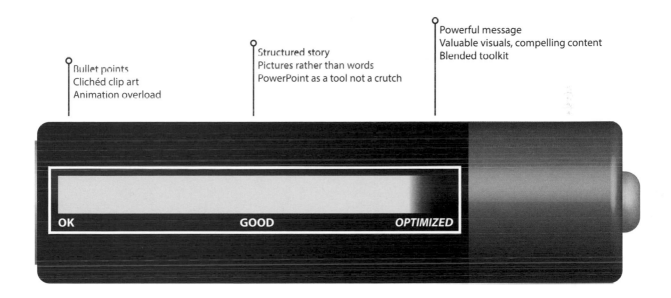

Bullet points
Clichéd clip art
Animation overload

Structured story
Pictures rather than words
PowerPoint as a tool not a crutch

Powerful message
Valuable visuals, compelling content
Blended toolkit

OK   GOOD   OPTIMIZED

Equipping yourself with a truly optimized presentation—that you can deliver in a host different ways—changes the game completely.

Audience engagement goes up a notch or three, your ability to influence and drive change increases, and all the hard work you put into getting to the presentation stage pays off.

Let's get cracking, eh?

THE PRESENTATION LAB

The Appliance of Science:
A Beginner's Guide

Element   A **B** C D E F G H

B₂

 ere is a vast amount of writing on presentations and their links to the innermost workings of the human brain. This is an opportunity for the aspiring presentation experts to get themselves embroiled in the complicated and occasionally confusing world of science.

For those with a yearning to "geek up," there are some well-trodden paths to follow:

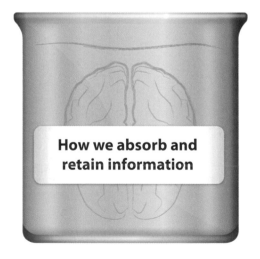

How we absorb and retain information

Remembering stuff

Professor Emeritus of Psychology Albert Mehrabian is perhaps the most commonly quoted expert in this area (see side panel). This expert on the relative importance of verbal and nonverbal messages does a good job in filling the "well, it's obvious when you think about it" void.

German psychologist Hermann Ebbinghaus works well here (see side panel). His theories on human memory provide a great deal of insight into how quickly people will forget most of what you have to say.

Albert Mehrabian, Professor Emeritus of Psychology at UCLA

Best known for his often-misquoted 7%-38%-55% rule. Mehrabian's study concluded that there are three elements in play when we figure out if we like someone when they share their feelings—the words used account for 7 percent, tone of voice accounts for 38 percent, and the remaining 55 percent is made up of body language.

Unfortunately, over time the rule has been mangled from its original focus on the 'like' engagement to acting as a scientific crutch for presentation experts looking to demonstrate the impact of placing too much text on a slide.

The big takeaway from Mehrabian's study is that communication is so much more than the words used—it's about the visual and auditory senses, too.

Hermann Ebbinghaus (1850–1909)

Best known for his "Forgetting Curve" hypothesis, which demonstrates the impact of time on people's ability to recall information (also known as transcience).

Importantly, for all business presenters, he identified that memory is also affected by how meaningful a subject matter is and how it is shared with an audience. Of particular interest in academic audiences is his suggestion that the use of mnemonics and repetition provide ways of improving memory.

As you may have picked up from my tone, I'm more than a little skeptical of much of the science that is thrown out to people looking to improve their presentations. This suspicion might sound a little peculiar coming from someone who chose to call their book *The Presentation Lab*, but there is good reason for it (honest). When we understand and apply it sympathetically, science can be an incredibly useful set of tools to have at our disposal. However, when we follow it slavishly, all common sense tends to leave the room—and you're left with an uninspiring and often meandering presentation and story.

I've seen some truly awful presentations developed for companies that tick all the boxes of scientific thinking. I guess it's one of the reasons that computers have never been able to create *true* art, such as poetry or music; we can never replace the human element in these things. The same goes for presentations.

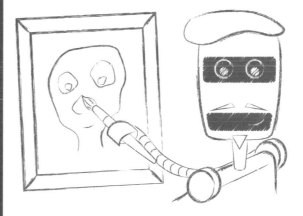

A computer may be able to beat you at chess (and, in my case, frequently does), but it'll never be able to create a story that engages and resonates with an audience like a human can, no matter how flawed that human may be.

Skepticism aside, I have found an amalgam of different scientific studies helpful in being able to apply labels to some things that we have seen work in the field with customers over the past nine years or so—Presentation Optimization.

The most relevant and easily applied of these many scientific insights was a comprehensive study by American psychologist, neuroscientist, author, and educator Stephen M. Kosslyn titled "Eight Cognitive Communication Principles" (catchy title, eh?). Because the study was initially designed to understand and analyze the flaws of PowerPoint and other presentation software, it provided a very nifty way of applying some science to three of the key stages of the Presentation Optimization methodology:

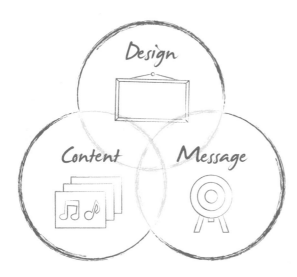

We'll revisit this study later on in the book.

What's the real purpose of applying science in presentations? Caveat Emptor

I've pondered this question numerous times and always reached the same couple of conclusions, all of which I've explained in detail below.

No need to learn through trial and error

There is a strong case to be made that all presentations should strongly follow psychology's guiding principles. After all, *presentation science* is merely the process of logging what happens naturally when we absorb information through a presenter and their visual tools. Surely, using these insights means we get it right more times than we get it wrong?

Does the application of science make it more likely that your next presentation will meet your objectives—specifically, in terms of making sure your audience understands your message and is moved sufficiently to take action? If so, get going—you're onto a winner. But in my experience, this is extremely unlikely. It's the equivalent of learning to ride a bike by reading a book about riding a bike. No matter how sufficiently you've researched, you'll end up falling off a few times before you get the knack—and the only way to figure that out is by *getting on the bike*. In other words, science is no replacement for getting out there.

Perhaps more important, presentations are about *connecting with people*. For all the rules, insight, and recommendations that science can bring, they can't guarantee that electric pulse that occurs between a presenter and their audience when a great presentation just *connects* everyone in the room. It's akin to when great writers, film directors, or musicians strive to create something that elicits that "spark"; rarely do they find it in the pages of a psychology book.

Justification

There's no doubt that it's easier to sell a new concept into a business if you're able to demonstrate its worth—particularly by referencing impartial but compelling evidence. *This* is where the science comes in for keen presentation thinkers and evangelists.

There's no getting away from it—some of the actions I'd like you to take after reading this book are a little, um, uncomfortable. Acting on concepts like corporate storytelling or Blended Presenting to your CEO are pretty nerve-wracking scenarios to consider. After all, they're probably more than comfortable with your current slide deck (heck, they're probably the ones who created it back in the day!). They're likely to perceive this new-fangled approach to presenting as being a little too fancy for them and their company.

But if you can add some science to the mix, you're able to quickly and (relatively) simply share the insights of very clever people who have a large number of letters after each of their names. Your CEO will be suitably impressed that you'd demonstrated the superhero levels of tenacity and enthusiasm to work through the long (and typically boring) theses you reference—and allow you to carry on as planned.

In conclusion

Whatever the reason for referencing the science that supports presentations, never make the mistake of believing that ticking all the psychology boxes will allow you to create and share something that will stick with your audience and inspire them into action. And *that's* the purpose of presenting in the first place.

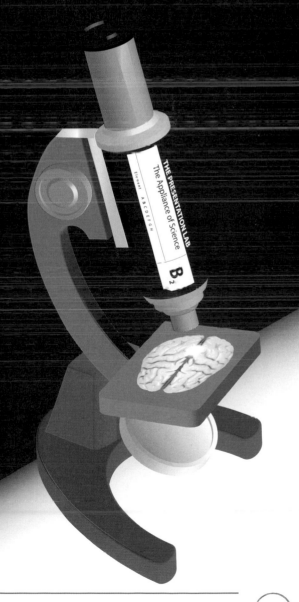

Element   A **B** C D E F G H

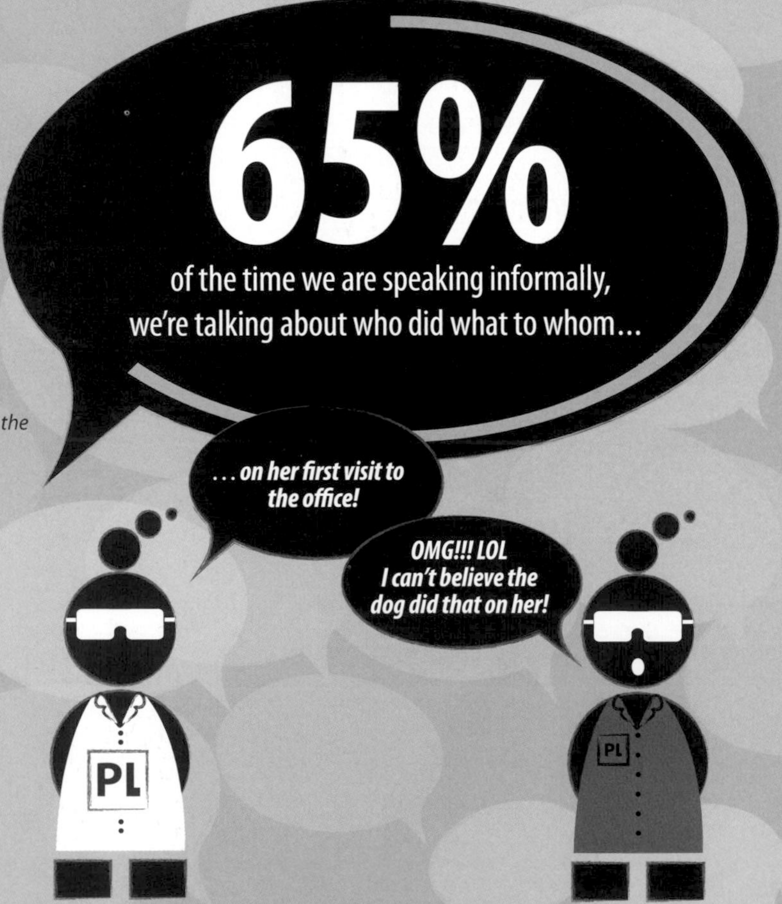

Dunbar, R. (1996)
*Grooming, Gossip, and the
Evolution of Language,
Harvard*

Clear, engaging, and ultimately successful business communication is vital. Without it, the cogs that drive business get gummed up and slowly but surely grind to a halt.

I witnessed it in my own business (oh, the irony) when the stresses of demanding customers, changing goalposts, and ever-tighter deadlines made working at Eyeful less than fun for a while.

The first casualty was communication—and in retrospect, the signs were there for all to see. People began resorting to e-mail more and more. This inevitably led to people misconstruing one another's e-mails more frequently, which resulted in some tense conversations. The consequence was that, in a frighteningly short period of time, key people were not really communicating or engaging with each other at all. It was horrible.

I knew I had to address the issue. So I did it with storytelling.

With so many people now dotted across the world, we had no alternative but to schedule a conference call. It is not my preferred method of communication, but necessity compelled us to do so.

We had no slides—no visuals whatsoever. I also set a limit of 10 minutes for the entire call.

I started by thanking people for joining the call and then recalled the vision I had for the business when I started it back in 2004: to build a company that would deliver the best possible presentation services to its customers through a mix of great people, smart thinking, and the need to ensure that each and every member of the team feels valued, respected, and engaged with the business.

I told a few short stories of how we convinced long-standing team members to join us in the first place—Sally over a cheap pizza in London, Liz through a series of increasingly bizarre interviews, and even having my dog pee on poor Vicki when she first visited the office. I spoke of the excitement we all felt when moving to our company headquarters, "Eyeful Towers," the peculiar novelty of our own dedicated server, and the buzz we all felt when winning each new customer.

I underlined that these everyday things defined "Eyefulocity" and made our company a special place to work. Our customers frequently commented that they felt this in the way we supported them and each other on projects. We were living the dream.

I then shared more recent and slightly less uplifting stories—when a team member was reduced to tears as a result of receiving an angry e-mail from a colleague; when a team felt demotivated by unrealistic deadlines; and the awful feeling of fear I had one morning when arriving at the office and sensing that we were slowly morphing into another "normal" company.

Ultimately the presentation was little more than a series of heartfelt but authentic stories . . .

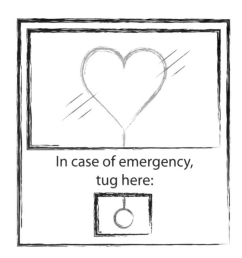

In case of emergency, tug here:

Stories that, frankly, I'd chosen to pull at my employees' heartstrings and make the audience feel the pain and disappointment I was feeling. It is easy to overlook the importance of authenticity in the stories I chose to share; they were stories that everyone could relate to immediately. The raw sense of disappointment expressed through the stories allowed the audience to reflect on how the changing behaviors described had affected the business's culture and their colleagues' and friends' happiness. With authenticity and emotion comes real power.

Without a solitary PowerPoint slide, the presentation touched everyone on that call and set the more positive agenda going forward. People still refer to the "Eyefulocity presentation" today as a crucial point in our business's development—one that, appropriately, relied totally on authentic storytelling.

Th ere are a lot of books that tell you how to tell a story, but most of them are incredibly complex and fairly confusing.

In general, stories don't need to be complex.

They simply need to follow a structure that gains interest, and then follow it up with sufficient emotion and engagement to keep the audience on board.

Let's consider the most basic of story structures:

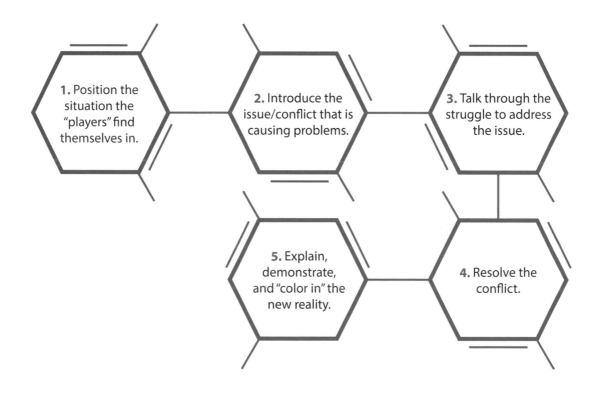

1. Position the situation the "players" find themselves in.

2. Introduce the issue/conflict that is causing problems.

3. Talk through the struggle to address the issue.

5. Explain, demonstrate, and "color in" the new reality.

4. Resolve the conflict.

Advertisers have used this approach for many years to sell their wares—and still do. Look out for tell-tale signs the next time you watch a TV ad.

For example, consider this commercial for shampoo:

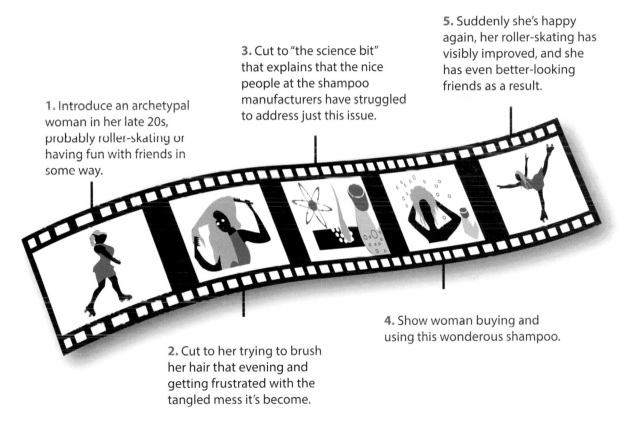

1. Introduce an archetypal woman in her late 20s, probably roller-skating or having fun with friends in some way.

2. Cut to her trying to brush her hair that evening and getting frustrated with the tangled mess it's become.

3. Cut to "the science bit" that explains that the nice people at the shampoo manufacturers have struggled to address just this issue.

4. Show woman buying and using this wonderous shampoo.

5. Suddenly she's happy again, her roller-skating has visibly improved, and she has even better-looking friends as a result.

Even though this example is a little tongue-in-cheek, you can see how the same structure can be used for all manners of different scenarios.

You can apply numerous story themes in a business environment, from the fantastical to the mundane but relevant. Here's a selection of personal favorites:

PICK YOURSELF UP AND START AGAIN

The Valiant Knight

THE ROAD TO DAMASCUS

THE EMPEROR'S NEW CLOTHES

DAVID & GOLIATH

Summary	Example	Optimal Usage
 The plucky individual or company that takes a hit but bounces back with aplomb and renewed vigor to win the day.	Steve Jobs bouncing back after being fired from his own company, Apple, and going on to lead Apple to astonishing success years later.	When looking to motivate a team into digging deep and finding the passion to try again—and succeed.
 Where either a company or an individual identifies that there is a problem and decides to do something—usually, something drastic and/or remarkable—about it.	The UK upstart "King of Shaves" taking on the might of Gillette and Wilkinson Sword in the tough men's toiletries sector or Richard Branson's Virgin brand competing with established airlines/banks/soft drink manufacturers (the list continues).	Perhaps in developing a new service or improving on a service that a lazy or unengaged incumbent provides.
The corporate equivalent of "seeing the light" and thinking and acting differently.	Perhaps it was a heavy industrial company who goes from pollutant to guardian of all things green or maybe a bank that wishes to conduct its business in a different manner.	Setting the scene for a brave new strategy and having the faith and commitment to see it through.

Summary	Example	Optimal Usage

| Using an example of where the corporate norm had become so engrained that change is almost impossible. | The invention of 3M's Post-it Note happened by accident—but rather than throwing it out, an individual saw the potential and persisted. | Empowering new employees/partners to drive fresh thinking and innovate from within the current confines of the organization. |

| The small company or individual who takes on a giant and wins through pure hard work, grit, determination, and skill. | Apple taking on the might of the recorded music industry and telephone handset industry through hard work and determination (and the iPhone, of course). | Demonstrating to a demotivated audience that hard work, commitment, and faith pay off and can change not only companies, but entire industries. |

Thankfully for presenters, the list of story themes is long and rich with opportunity. It's also crucial to remember that you shouldn't limit these themes to purely business situations; some of the most lucid and engaging stories are those from our childhood or family life. If they work and support your message, grab them with both hands.

Your audience deserves your best material, so don't be shy. Use every weapon in your storytelling arsenal to get your message across.

The Basic Tools for the Job

"The UNIVERSE IS MADE OF STORIES, NOT ATOMS."

Muriel Rukeyser
American Poet & Activist

THE PRESENTATION LAB
Introducing Presentation Optimization

B5

Element   A **B** C D E F G H

One of the most important but, in truth, least glamorous stages of developing a presentation is the planning stage. It's vital to get your ducks in a row early on, because you set yourself up for a fall if you dive into a presentation without the required preparation.

At Eyeful Presentations, we use a methodology called Presentation Optimization to ensure we don't miss any essential content or, perhaps more important, skip any steps. Presentation Optimization has evolved over a number of years and, like any good process, is constantly checked and tweaked to ensure it remains valuable and viable for our customers and consultants to use.

I remember when it "came of age" in the very early days of Eyeful after we had "stress tested" it within an inch of it's very young life.

Picture the scene:

Many, many years ago, I received a phone call from a large international hotel chain. This was in the very early days of Eyeful, so it was rare to receive any phone calls, let alone one from an international brand like this. Despite this, I answered the phone as if this is what I did everyday (call it salesmanship).

The chap on the other end of the phone was lovely—really engaging and full of enthusiasm for his new project. He explained that the hotel chain was looking to expand its network of franchised hotels and had developed a presentation for it's executive team to use to convince external parties to invest. The only problem was that while the presentation was aesthetically very pleasing, it wasn't performing in the way that they had hoped.

Massive International Hotel Chain
Calling…

Answer

I asked him to e-mail the slides to me and said that I'd review for him, prepare some feedback and ideas, and perhaps pop into their offices for a coffee and a chat later that week. He explained that the file was too large to e-mail so he'd arrange for a courier to send it around "to your studio." (Little did he know I was speaking to him from our spare bedroom in a very nice but not particularly "media city–style" suburban street outside of Oxford).

After frantically dashing around trying to make the outside of our house look "studio like," the courier turned up with a beautifully packaged CD.

With a fair amount of trepidation, I loaded the CD into the computer and sat slack-jawed as one gorgeous, impeccably crafted slide after another appeared on the screen. The artwork and animation were things of beauty and prompted just two questions in my mind: How the hell was I going to add *any value* to this masterpiece? And what the heck was I going to chat about with him later that week?

After the rising sense of panic slowly subsided, I took a second, closer look at this work of presentation art . . . and actually started to spot a couple of areas that I would change. None of this had to do with the presentation's look and feel; rather, it had everything to do with the message and content of their story.

Summarized, their story went as follows:

We're really big and successful.

No really, you don't understand—we're huge. You're lucky to even be in the same room as us.

These are our terms of working together.

DEAL?

They were portraying their message in the worst possible ways—from kicking off the presentation with an organizational chart that prominently featured their company's Most Important People (including pictures and microscopic text), followed by page after page of charts depicting growth and success for the very clever people who ran this international business.

Not one slide mentioned the issues, opportunities, or aspirations of the equally successful audience! The more I reviewed and looked beyond the fancy slides, the more I realized what a train wreck of a presentation it actually was. And I went from being petrified of meeting with the prospect to being excited.

Finally the time came to visit the hotel chain's headquarters. I duly prepared for a nice quiet chat over coffee to share my thoughts and ideas on how we could improve the presentation. My approach was to make it informal with no finger pointing or big gestures. To me, this was all about supporting a new friend in tweaking some of their content.

This led to my next surprise. Upon my arrival, my contact came around the corner, shook my hand warmly, and uttered those immortal lines: "The other guys are just finishing their pitch and then the board will be ready for you."

Gulp.

They expected a pitch?! The board?! I had come with a "steam-driven" laptop, some basic feedback, and a handful of doodles—no more. Indeed, with this being so early on in the life of Eyeful, if they had wanted a full pitch, I wouldn't have had much more to pull upon.

Thinking of my wife and newly born daughter and the knowledge that I'd have to earn some money to feed them at some point, I entered the room. A group of frankly grumpy-looking middle-aged men faced me in an intimidating horseshoe of desks and told me to set up my personal computer and take them through my concepts.

"Well, actually, I'd rather share with you my feedback on the current presentation first," I croaked while simultaneously wondering, "What samples can I show them" and "Where is the nearest exit?"

I took a deep breath and displayed their current deck while highlighting a few concerns. I asked them about their audience and why they thought kicking off with an organizational chart of their business was a good idea. I followed up by asking some simple questions about what was important to their audience. I also emphasized the fact that if they were very lucky, they could be seen as a small cog in a big machine—the franchised part of the business was renowned for looking after its franchisees and had delivered great returns for all that had gotten involved.

The questions kept flowing and the board's uncertain (or was it impatient?) shuffling increased. Finally, the biggest and scariest member of the board brought my line of questioning to a halt by slamming his fist down onto the desk and exclaiming,

"Thank £$&% for that!"

"I've wasted the past 3 hours listening to creative types telling me what they can do with my PowerPoint template and logo—but you're the first person to actually point out what's wrong with the presentation.

We're not communicating the way we should. It shouldn't be about us; it should be about our audience.

"When can you start?"

I arranged a time for a full consultation workshop, shuffled out of the room as quickly as I could, and went to lie down.

What followed was a pretty intense series of workshops, visual redesign (we agreed less was more), and the development of a completely new presentation story. I'm pleased to say our customer grew the franchise side of their business and, nine years down the line, we continue to work closely with people across the group (even the scary board members).

But more important, from this experience, Presentation Optimization was born. We now had a methodology that allowed us to look beyond the aesthetics and really hone in on the important stuff: the message, the use of valuable content, and the need to always keep the audience top of mind.

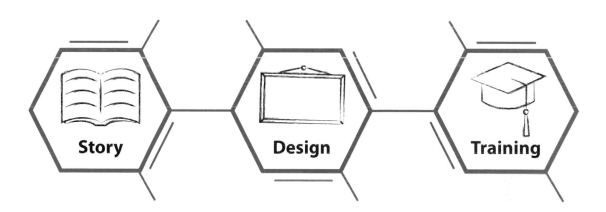

Story   **Design**   **Training**

It's a methodology that we've since used on thousands of presentations for companies large and small across the globe. No matter what people have thrown at it over the years—from workshops in Russian via an interpreter to late night storyboarding sessions—it's remained robust and agile enough to cope. Truth be told, we're rather proud of it and it's achievements over the past nine or so years.

That said, it will continue to be a work in progress for many years to come as new technologies, new external factors (online, the proliferation of social media as a feedback channel), and new experiences all come along to influence our thinking. In fact, perhaps the most important thing we've learned from our approach is that nothing's ever set in stone.

There are, however, some constants . . . the audience and the need for a powerful and engaging story.

THE PRESENTATION LAB

The Base Elements of Your Presentation

C

Element   A B **C** D E F G H

THE PRESENTATION LAB
The Base Elements of Your Presentation

Element   A B **C** D E F G H

The concept of *The Presentation Lab* is not one I've casually thrown together to create a snappy title for a book. Akin to developing a new drug, creating a presentation demands meticulous planning and preparation along with some serious brainpower. There must be sufficient controls in place to guard against things getting out of hand.

The two core elements of your presentation development process are:

1. **A thorough understanding of your audience**

2. **Clarity on what your message is**

If you can master these concepts, both you and your presentation will be in good shape going forward. If you rush or try to short cut this section, it will be at your peril.

The good news is that once these elements are firmly in place, we can really go to town in terms of finessing the content, polishing the visuals, and preparing to actually deliver the presentation to your audience. But we're getting ahead of ourselves. Let's focus on that all important element of your presentation formula: the **audience**.

Respect the Audience

C_2

Element   A B **C** D E F G H

The more you think about it, the more obvious it is.

Every presentation represents an investment the audience is making in you. It accounts for the obvious stuff like time and attention, but it also includes something a little more entrancing: their willingness to connect with you and your story.

There's no getting away from it; it's a huge privilege to be able to present something to a group of people.

Yet despite the audience's investment, we all too often see presenters who have scant regard for their audiences. They simply "roll up" and deliver the same precanned, half-baked presentation that not only fails to interest the audience but also, thanks to the presenter's tone and approach, bores them, too.

A presentation is an incredible opportunity to really connect with each individual member of the audience. It is often the net result of a huge amount of hard work to get to the point of presenting (reference "The Presentation Paradox" on page 19). Presenters have spent hours, days, weeks, sometimes even months planning, jostling, and positioning to get in front of the right audience. Yet, despite this, people seem happy to throw away this hard work when they are given this incredible opportunity.

Treat your audience with the utmost respect. They are opening themselves and their minds up to your message. They probably don't need to be there, and chances are, they have a whole bunch of other interesting and pressing stuff to be doing. Yet they chose to invest their time, energy, and attention in you.

Even if you have a "captive audience" (internal presentations are a classic example of this—legions of employees sitting in a darkened room wishing they were somewhere else), don't make the mistake of thinking that they *have* to be there. True; you can force them to be there in body. But the real investment is in their attention, their willingness to engage in spirit, and ultimately embrace your message.

You cannot afford to dismiss **any** audience. The best route is to value and respect the opportunity they are giving you—because it's immense.

Respect for Audience

Respect from Audience

Audiences:
The Most Complex of Beasts…

C₃

Element   A   B **C** D E F G H

Once you understand the value and importance of your audience, you can then move on to the tricky business of understanding them and how they tick. Tricky, yes, but vital in ensuring you deliver *true* presentation success.

Each presentation represents an involved courtship between presenter and audience. Like any relationship, it requires "give and take" and emotional investment from both sides to make it work.

Get this mix right, and the presenter and the presentation fly. Suddenly, it's simple and a joy to be involved in. However, should you get the tone of your presentation wrong, the bond between presenter and audience vanishes into thin air, causing things to go awry very quickly. An audience can turn on you or, even worse, switch off completely, bringing any seasoned presenter to their knees.

So why is this engagement with an audience so fraught with danger and anxiety? It primarily comes down to the inconvenient truth that they tend to consist of people.

And as anyone who has ever been in a relationship, raised children, been a child themselves, or generally "existed" will acknowledge, people are complex beasts. Take a moment to think about your family or groups of friends and colleagues. By their very nature, they will consist of a complex mass of opinions, backgrounds, ages, motives, and beliefs. Presentation audiences are exactly the same.

Yet despite this smorgasbord of personality influences, it is incumbent on us as presenters to connect with our audience members quickly and effectively each and every time we sit down with them. It's nothing short of a mind-blowing undertaking.

This leaves your Average Joe business presenter with an interesting dilemma. Do they try and untangle the complex web of personalities for each and every presentation, analyzing and fine tuning their content, visuals, and style to address the needs of this carefully profiled audience? Or, do they create a presentation that takes a sufficiently broad-brush approach to the whole subject on the assumption that by not shocking or upsetting anyone, they've at least "got away with it"?

One of the easiest mistakes to make in presenting is to assume that business audience personalities are formed directly in line with people's job functions. Not all marketing people are zany with wacky spectacles, not all CEOs are short tempered tyrants, and not all finance people are detail-oriented geeks.

Although presenters might do this with the very best of intentions, the end result is that they play directly to clichés and stereotypes—rather than real people. We owe it to our audiences to think beyond the stereotype and consider them as individual personalities.

One assumes that presenters have gathered sufficient knowledge of the audience members before stepping in front of them. And this is possible in a perfect, well-planned, and carefully project managed world. However, it is rarely the case in reality. The other is nothing short of a cop-out: Make the presentation content generic enough to ensure no one is offended or feels left out. This is like making an action movie but cutting out the exciting bits to ensure it gets a PG rating. In short, it's a terrible idea.

In the end, the best approach sits somewhere in the middle: Cultivate a presentation that acknowledges the different personality types that comprise an audience, one that possesses sufficient content and flexibility to address their specific needs while also being universal enough to be used time and time again. This is going to be more valuable—both to you as the presenter and, more important, to your audience. The value here is not just about ensuring that you get your message across clearly and powerfully; it's also about demonstrating the most rare of things in many business presentations: respect for the audience (see page 56).

At this point, it's awfully tempting to get into a lot of very clever science and psychology, calling upon Jung, Freud, and the like to explain how people interact, think, and operate. I could spend the next 20 pages waxing lyrical about the left brain and right brain, mulling over the importance of rationale versus instinct and, frankly, confusing and boring most readers. The Presentation Lab is about equipping you with practical skills and not bombarding you with quite interesting, but not entirely useful, theory.

Instead, I'd like us to focus on a simple but powerful way of splitting your audience into groups based on personality types instead of job function.

Geek

Emotional

Zany

Creative

Serious

Cool

**Personality
Types**

At a very basic level, most business audiences can be split into three groups:

 Factual

Data matters for this group. They'll make decisions based on cold hard facts over anything fluffier. They want to know about return on investment (ROI), improvement in performance, and how they can add value to the bottom line.

If the story stacks up on an Excel spreadsheet or structured business plan, chances are that they'll listen to you and your message carefully. If it doesn't, they'll quickly disengage and wait quietly and politely for the presentation to finish.

 Emotional

People in this group are driven by their heart first and their head second. Emotional does not always equate to positive; if they don't "feel" good about your message or approach, they'll shut down quickly and relatively irrationally.

There is a sense of volatility to this sort of audience. They are quick to form opinions, normally in the absence of any firm data to back it up, and will usually stick to these assertions. Once you've established that emotional bond, good or bad, it takes a lot to change their initial response.

 Visionary

Seeing the big picture is important to this group. They are people who ponder, consider a broad range of factors, and then apply them more widely than most.

They hungrily devour well-thought-out benefit statements, will grab hold of detailed case studies, and show an active interest in what the future holds for your idea. By the same token, they'll have to fight the temptation to switch off if you get dragged into the detail around costs, ROI, or implementation processes.

It's all too tempting to start assigning typical business roles to each of these personalities—the finance person as the Factual one, the marketing guy as the Emotional one, and the CEO as the Visionary—but the reality is somewhat different. The fact is that most individuals tend to be a mix of all three—albeit in different quantities—and the same applies to grouped audiences. I know some very emotional finance people and some incredibly analytical marketing people. Like it is with most scenarios, the stereotypes don't work.

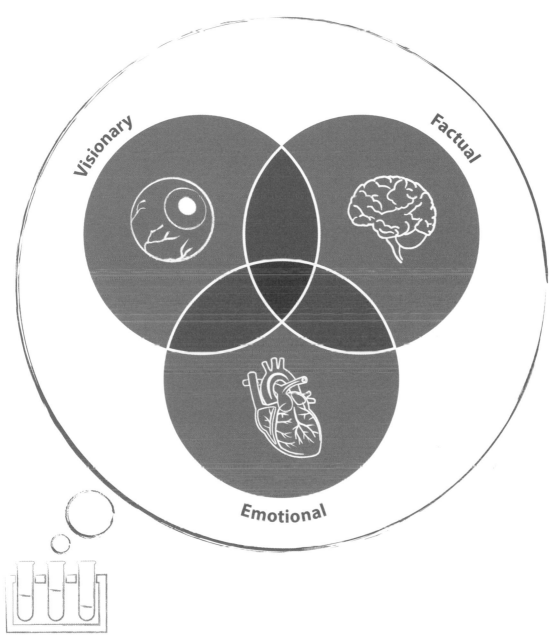

Identifying these personality types helps determine how they interact with one another (and you as the presenter) in different situations. I have worked with a vast array of business presenters and audiences over the years and seen how the formula changes from one presentation type to another. Awareness of these shifting group dynamics has allowed us to develop a "heat map" visual when preparing for different presentation audiences. As you would expect, the heat map shifts in line with a number of variables, from the type of presentation you're delivering through to the sector you may be working in.

Presentation Purpose: Credentials Presentation

Presentation Type: Persuasive

Sector: Environmental Solution

A large proportion of the projects we work on at Eyeful Presentations fall into the "credentials presentation" space. These are business-to-business (B2B) presentations that we typically develop for field-based teams to use as part of their face-to-face sales process.

As such, the audiences that they engage with can vary wildly, from the very Factual for our pharma and medical customers to more emotive for business services. We'll occasionally work with a start-up or extremely entrepreneurial business that is breaking new ground and needs a credentials presentation to allow them to position themselves as thought leaders or market makers.

We did a recent project for a local company who had developed a unique way of recycling previously "toxic" materials such as diapers and other sanitary materials. They were using some very clever science to turn them into plastic goods such as park benches and (ironically) recycling bins. It was a tremendously exciting project to be involved in. Not only was the company looking to address an ongoing problem (diapers in landfill sites), but it was also finding new ways of using the output.

It would have seemingly been easy to put the company's solution firmly in the warm and fuzzy box due to the impact of their unique process. But the reality was very different—and determined directly by their audience. They were initially presenting to a group of "green ambassadors," procurement, and CEOs from hospitals and local authorities across the United Kingdom. Although there's no doubt that these people had some level of interest in the great green story surrounding the process, their real focus was much more cut and dry:

- How could this save them ever-increasing waste disposal costs?

- How would this help them address the public outcry at the amount of waste being dumped in local landfill sites?

- How could they use this service to further their own profile and standing among their peers (and thus attract additional funding from central government)?

As such, the "audience heat map" we developed differed from what you may have initially thought. It was far less emotionally charged than we had anticipated—the Factual and Visionary elements came through very strongly as the business case and future opportunities were discussed:

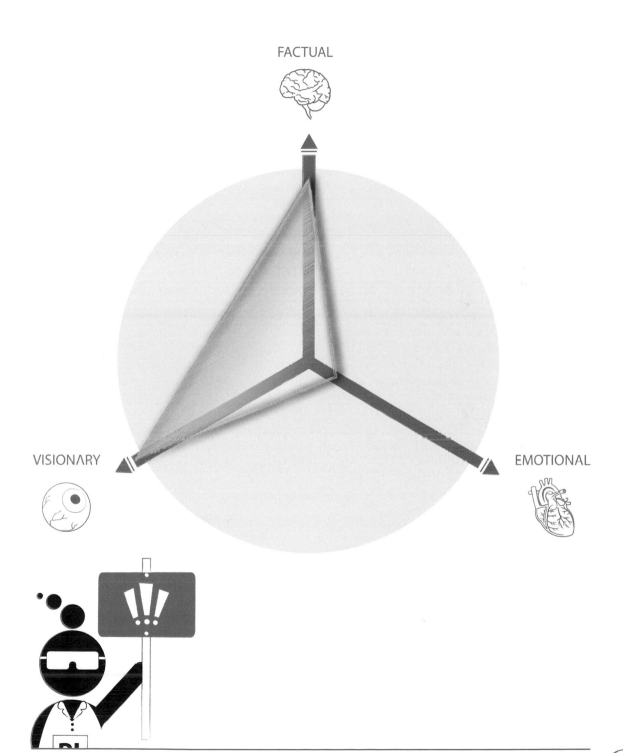

FACTUAL

VISIONARY

EMOTIONAL

Presentation Purpose: Internal Change

Presentation Type: Informative

Sector: Global Software

We also worked on project for an international software provider. Following a number of credentials presentation projects, this organization approached us to work on a sensitive project. After acquiring a smaller competitor, management was looking to lose just under 15 percent of the workforce as they consolidated the two companies.

The company shared many of the internal characteristics of businesses in this sector—it was full of smart, well paid, and frankly, opinionated individuals. As such, sharing news around any sort of restructure was fraught with danger—most obviously an immediate impact on morale, but also the potential for public relations (PR) headaches as the news was leaked to the industry.

Again, we looked beyond the obvious when reviewing the audience profile. Although it was primarily comprised of Factual individuals (working in software can do that to you), the presentation's nature would certainly elicit an emotional response. We also needed to address the "big picture" to paint a positive and ultimately upbeat picture for those employees remaining.

The "audience heat map" changed to reflect the nature of the message plus the volatility of the people in the room. In turn, this allowed us to develop the tone of voice for the presentation accordingly: As shown in the diagram opposite, to demonstrate the logical reasoning behind the decision while addressing the inevitable emotional impact it would have on the audience.

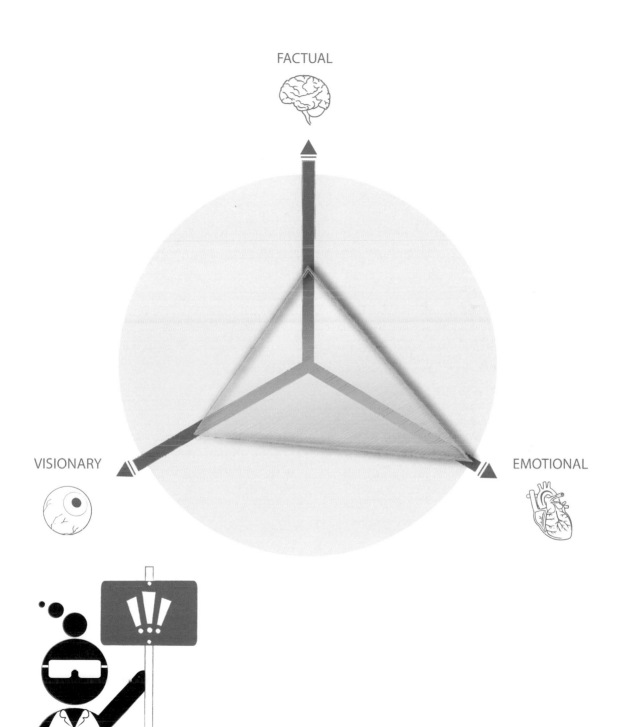

Presentation Purpose: Investor Relations

Presentation Type: Informative

Sector: Private Equity

Before we started working with Private Equity companies, I'll gladly confess to not really understanding how they worked. The first few presentations we worked on were little more than "lipstick on a pig"—type projects, where there seemed to be more focus on making charts look pretty than supporting a sustained message. But after a while, we started to understand more about the audience we were developing slides for—and ultimately determined how to improve the approach.

Our customer's goal was for its investors to learn more about what made each of their fund companies tick. To achieve this, they'd get the various CEOs to stand up and share their story—from the eureka moment through to painting a picture of what the future holds. On paper, it looked like a great way to show the big picture and add color to something that had the potential to be a presentation dominated by charts and data. The problem was that some of the CEOs took this as an opportunity to share their life stories, ultimately delivering an Emotional style of presentation. This led to an unfortunate mismatch between the presentation and audience.

The audience at an investor forum is made up of very clever people. I mean *really* clever; they can review an earnings before interest, taxes, depreciation, and amoritzation (EBITDA) forecast chart and draw a well thought out and considered conclusion at 50 paces. It's really quite remarkable.

And in addition to being very smart, they're also *extremely* busy. They're constantly checking their mobile devices—not as a slight to the presenter, but because they truly do need to be 'on it' the entire time. They simply don't have time to get Emotional as each of the presentations is delivered. For them, it's all about the facts.

The diagram should give you a pretty good picture of the people sitting in the auditorium. They are here to understand the short-term business case behind decisions while getting a long-term understanding of opportunities for each of the companies.

With this in mind, we toned down the presentation's Emotional content and focused on the Factual (obviously). We also coached the CEO presenters to engage with the Visionary part of the audience psyche. This was the exciting part and, more important, humanized the presentation without being too emotional. It quickly became a Unique Selling Point for this event and our customer.

FACTUAL

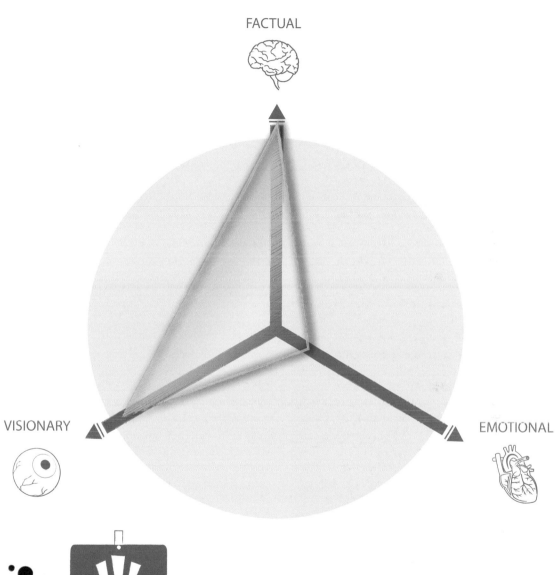

VISIONARY   EMOTIONAL

Presentation Purpose: Persuasive

Presentation Type: Bid

Sector: IT Services

The high stakes surrounding bid presentations can take the nervous presenter dangerously off-track very quickly. Many will ditch the concept of 'playing to the audience' and use this presentation as an excuse to simply regurgitate the same structure and content that's in the original tender document.

It's an easy trap to fall into. And it's one that could potentially cost you that high profile and profitable contract.

One of our longest-standing customers is a U.S.-based information technology (IT) company responsible for delivering mission-critical services into the financial services sector. It is a massively successful organization, something we can attribute to a variety of factors: continued dominance among competitors, the quality of its services (failure is simply unthinkable), and the staff's "can-do" attitude.

This IT company was asked to bid on a project for which it would be providing some very complex services to run the back room processing for a high-profile global bank. The sales staff had run the gauntlet of numerous meetings, audits, and bid submissions over the previous 24 months—all of which culminated in a crunch time presentation.

We spent the early stage of the development process carefully reviewing the named audience members, their responsibilities, and our customer's existing relationship with them. The more the project team discussed the audience, the more obvious it became that the bid's success centered on **trust**. Our customer could technically deliver the solution without breaking into too much of a sweat; the same went for their two nearest competitors. They could distinguish themselves from the competition by demonstrating that the bank could trust them to deliver on the project scope—and that they would be easier to work with.

It was time to engage and play to the audience's Emotional facets, while aligning these to the factual box-ticking elements required to connect with the professionals in the room. It's important to note that this focus on the Emotional and Factual audience drivers does not exclude the Visionary element; the audience wanted to know that there was an element of future-proofing in place. However, previous meetings, audits, and documents had addressed much of this.

The presentation we created for this "must-win" bid successfully demonstrated trust and a shared vision for how the project should be run. This, in conjunction with keen pricing, an enviable reputation, and some great account management, contributed to our customer winning one of the largest orders in their long history.

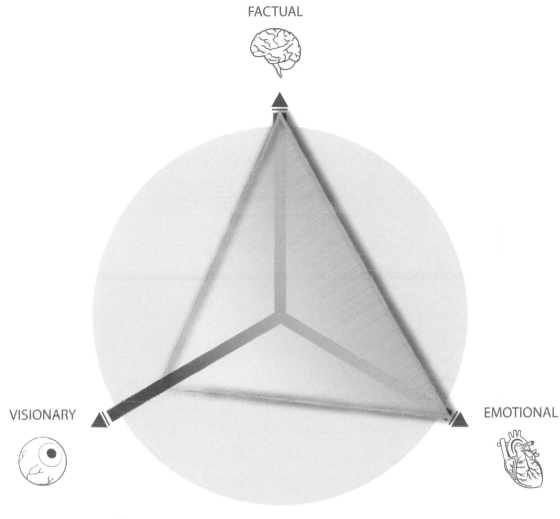

FACTUAL

VISIONARY

EMOTIONAL

Drawing Conclusions

Understanding the different forces in play within audiences makes life a lot simpler and more efficient when creating presentations. It also makes the "presentation scientist" aware of the pitfalls inherent in assuming that stereotypes of different job functions or presentation type are a guide upon which you can base your approach.

It is the presentation creator's responsibility to think and go deeper.

So what does this mean to us as presentation creators and deliverers? Pretty much everything: You dismiss your audience and its profile at your peril. Showing up and delivering the same tone of presentation to a range of different audiences is a recipe for disaster. It's the equivalent of booking the same entertainment for a bachelor party and the subsequent wedding reception. These are clearly two different audiences who require two different types of engagement. When you assume that one size fits all, you run the risk of either disappointing—or, in the case of the bachelor/wedding party, upsetting—more than a few members of your audience.

This audience profile needs to be paramount in your mind when creating your presentation. The people to whom you're presenting should form the basis of some very basic questions:

 Message

- What is your message, and how do you anticipate the audience will react to it?
- What is a realistic expectation of them following the presentation?
- What do you want them to do as a result of hearing your message?

 Content

- What kind of tone and language will resonate with them?
- What do they already know?
- What don't they know that you might have to provide some background on?

 Delivery

- What are the right presentation tools for the job?
- How can you use visuals to connect with them?

Different audiences demand (and deserve!) different approaches. Because these varied approaches share the same basic presentation building blocks—message, content, and design—you need to apply them in line with your audience. An Emotional audience won't benefit from too much data, a Visionary audience requires "big-picture" statements, and the Factual will need more detail than most.

Get the mix right and you have a strong and robust foundation in place to build upon. Make too many assumptions or fall into the trap of believing stereotypes, and you run the risk of losing your audience before you've even started.

So armed with an understanding of your audience profile, how do you take this and evolve it into a structure that meets their demands? It's time to introduce the Audience Pathway…

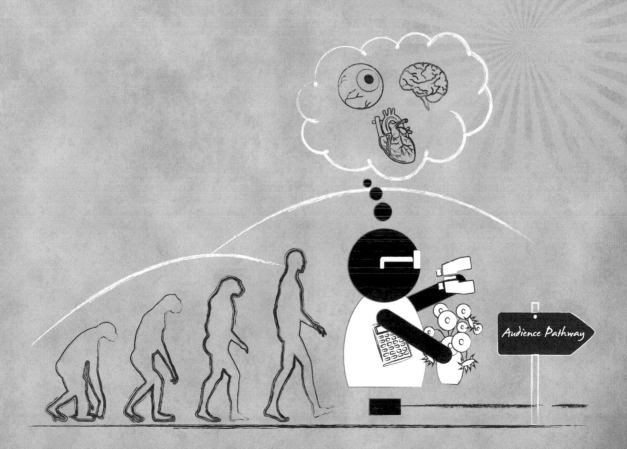

The Audience Pathway

C₄

Element   A B **C** D E F G H

All of this understanding and empathizing with your audience is all very nice, of course. But to what end? What's our intended result, and just how are we going to get them there?

No matter what mix of audience types you're facing—be they predominantly Emotional, Factual, or Visionary—they all need to **take a journey** from the initial faltering steps through to wholehearted action. Your job as the presenter is to guide them through this journey as quickly and painlessly as possible.

Your audience needs to take a pathway made up of four distinct phases, shown in the graphic below:

Audience Pathway

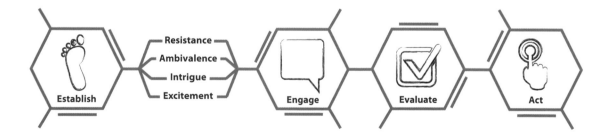

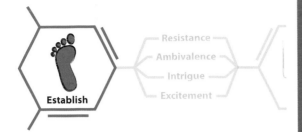

Of all four stages, *Establish* perhaps comes with the highest stakes. You can see on the diagram above that there are a few things coming between this and the next step of *Engage*. This phase is where the skeptics, the cynics, and the downright disruptive will raise their heads and ruthlessly disrupt the presentation. They might express this through body language (crossed arms accompanied with a dramatic sigh are never a good sign) or by asking loaded questions that demonstrate to the rest of the audience that they don't want to be there. Although visions of strangling the members of the audience involved might seem cathartic, it is better to recognize their resistance as part of the process. You need to establish the reason they *are* in the room and use this to frame the engagement going forward.

This takes a very negative view of the *Establish* phase, however. It's somewhat of a worst case scenario. More often than not, this phase is a positive one and more about managing the audience's interest, intrigue, and excitement. Again, recognizing that this is merely the start of the process allows you to plan your presentation structure carefully to ensure your audience's good intentions are duly respected.

The aim at this stage is a simple one: keep them on your side, get them all on the same page, and proceed as quickly as you can to the *Engage* stage.

The general ignorance to this phase is the reason so many standard "Death by PowerPoint" corporate presentations fail. Kicking off a long deck of bullet point–strewn slides with pictures of your office building, an organizational chart, or your financial performance is a red rag to a bull at this stage of the Audience Pathway. Slides like this give individuals looking to mentally check out early a license to do exactly that.

This is why the structure and story of your presentation is so important: They allow you to grab the audience's attention and work with it until they are properly engaged. Failure to do so will mean you've lost your audience—or never had them in the first place—rendering the entire presentation pretty much pointless. No pressure, then…

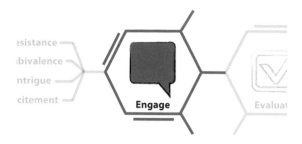

Engage

Evaluat

The *Engage* stage is where all the magic happens. It's where your compelling content, coupled with your valuable visuals, work seamlessly to support the message that resonates loud and clear with your audience. It's the phase where your emotional audience members fall in (or out of) love with you and your message. It's where the factual ones start to take on board the content you're sharing, and it's where the visionaries in the room see the cogs start turning as the bigger picture slowly starts to come into focus.

Engaging your audience is a wonderful experience. Professional speakers will talk misty eyed about the second they knew they had the audience in the palm of their hands—that special moment when the entire room was on the same page. It's very easy for us mere mortals who don't make their living presenting to enraptured crowds to think that this 'magical moment' is out of our reach. The cynics might say that taking inspiration from great orators like Steve Jobs, Dr. Martin Luther King, or Winston Churchill is fine—but the reality is different. For them, getting through the presentation unscathed, with reputation intact and the audience still awake is a win.

Beware—this kind of thinking is a sign that you're selling yourself short, very short.

Make no mistake: Business presentations provide as much opportunity to create magic moments as the big-ticket speeches by Steve, Dr. King, and Winston. The reason we drag out and cite these examples so regularly is that they are great exponents of **audience engagement**, not because of the oratory skills, grandeur of the venue, or the eye-popping visuals that were on display. (In fact, rumor has it that Churchill was rubbish at PowerPoint.)

If you boil it all down, engaging your audience is remarkably, almost embarrassingly, simple; It's just a matter of taking time to get the basics right. It's very much the same as engaging and building a relationship with someone new. You put yourself in the other person's shoes, show interest in the things that are bugging that person, and demonstrate that you understand—and that you might ultimately be able to help the person. It really is as simple as the old "What's in it for me?" (WIIFM) sales 101 training most business professionals have undergone. We all know it, but rarely follow it through.

Engage　　　　**Evaluate**　　　　Act

This leads rather nicely on to the *Evaluate* phase. This principally involves you spelling out the impact your proposition will have and then allowing your audience to chew it over before forming their own opinion. Depending on your audience's profile, this might entail them processing hard return on investment (ROI) facts that demonstrate the logical reason for proceeding with the plan. It might mean allowing them the time to mull over your carefully constructed benefit statements ("what this means to you"). Either way, you need to ensure that you give your audience time to process your message. This investment in evaluation will prompt questions which ultimately will give you a further springboard to demonstrate your understanding and passion for the project. Done correctly, it's a win-win for both you and the audience.

As mentioned previously, it's all too easy to think of the Audience Pathway as a single linear process. Odds are, you'll need to provide some clarification or discuss particularly complex issues in more detail. In these instances, you may find you need to take the audience through the *Engage–Evaluate* process a number of times. This is when it's invaluable to equip yourself with a flexible presentation tool (or ideally tools); they allow you to build to the crescendo of the *Act* phase.

Sometimes taking a few small bites at the cherry is the best way to get to your goal. There is no need to rush things!

I'm not a big fan of the ubiquitous, "Any Questions?" slide that plagues most corporate presentations. To me, it smacks of an artificial engagement with the audience, the subtext being, "You may now speak."

If you took this approach at a networking event or at an internal meeting, you'd be left out in the cold very quickly. Yet it seems to have become the norm in business presentations. A well-paced and carefully structured presentation should allow the audience to proffer questions **along the way** as part of the *Evaluate* phase, rather than granting them a chance at the end—if there's time.

Remarkably, the most common absence from the business presentations I am asked to "Healthcheck" is a clear **Call to Action**. It's a most peculiar trait that seems to affect presentations from companies large and small and from all over the world. People seem to either forget (unlikely) or feel uncomfortable asking their audience to take some sort of action at the conclusion of their presentation.

This is incredibly confusing, of course—because the ultimate purpose of presenting is to *prompt an action or a change* from your audience. It might come in the form of them spending money with you, approving a new approach or simply thinking differently. But the action doesn't really matter if you don't ask the question and prompt the audience to respond!

The trick in any successful and joined up presentation is to make the Call to Action as natural as possible by working *with* the audience profile rather than against it. Going for a hard close to a room full of Emotional people will do nothing to aid your cause, and being too high level and fluffy with a Factual audience will do you no favors either.

It makes no sense to go to the trouble of developing a presentation around a specific Audience Pathway without including a Call to Action. Not only does it waste your time, but it wastes your audience's, too—which is even worse. Without it, you fail to demonstrate that all-important respect for your audience. (And if you're questioning this advice at this point, might I respectfully suggest you read Section C again. It really is *that* important!)

The Base Elements of Your Presentation

This topic reminds me of a job interview I had early on in my career. I was going for a sales position with a multinational telecoms firm and the role was more than a few steps up the corporate ladder from what I was currently doing. After a few rounds of initial telephone and panel interviews, I was invited to present to the UK board on the art of sales.

Put nicely, the chap to whom I would be reporting if I got the job was a walking, talking business-to-business sales cliché. He was all about winning the deal at any cost, pushing, and closing as much as possible, a real "coffee's for closers"* kind of guy.

After my short presentation (that included a very clear call to action), we got into a discussion about closing:

- What techniques did I use to close deals?

- What did I believe was the art of the close?

- Perhaps the most alarming of all: **How fast can you close?**

This prompted quite a detailed discussion around the structure of a sales presentation, including my strongly held belief that the close should never come as a surprise to a prospect. The entire presentation structure, the engagement with the different audience types, and the positioning of the proposition should all be designed to lead to the point where the prospect takes action.

It's final stage of the Audience Pathway; we pass the baton over to them, and they then need (and hopefully by that point, *want*) to Act.

My potential future boss and I debated this approach long and hard. He saw my response as a cop-out; I saw it as professional salesmanship. His bosses agreed with me, and I got the job. Interestingly, I left within three months because of the questionable sales tactics that this company employed (but only after becoming their highest earner that quarter).

*Those who don't recognize this reference should check out the amazing movie *Glengarry Glen Ross* when you get a chance. It's extraordinary, especially for those of us who have a background in sales.

Navigating Your Way along the Pathway

Understanding the steps along the pathway is important, but it's primarily a matter of common sense. The real power comes from knowing how to *apply* each of these stages to the different audience profiles, from the use of emotive language through to the application of visuals, data, and different Calls to Action.

The following diagram provides a high-level view of how to engage different audience profiles at each of the Audience Pathway steps.

As always, remember that these are not mutually exclusive. You're still able to drive the engagement stage of the presentation with a predominantly emotional audience by using charts (just don't overdo it!). In much the same way, building rapport with an audience is a valuable thing to do with *all* manner of different groups. You just may find that it's more efficient to cut to the chase to demonstrate knowledge when speaking to a predominantly Factual audience.

Ultimately this diagram is designed to offer a rule of thumb for structuring your presentation to meet the predominant audience profile.

Audience Pathway
Presentation tone of voice

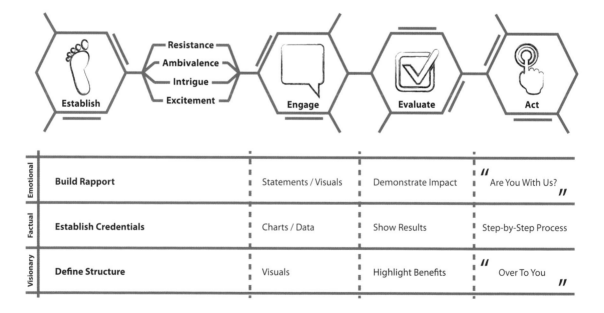

	Establish	Engage	Evaluate	Act
Emotional	Build Rapport	Statements / Visuals	Demonstrate Impact	" Are You With Us? "
Factual	Establish Credentials	Charts / Data	Show Results	Step-by-Step Process
Visionary	Define Structure	Visuals	Highlight Benefits	" Over To You "

Audiences with a strong Emotional scale want to feel that they are on a journey with you, hence, the *Act* phase being an inclusive "Are you with us?" Such an informal approach at the conclusion of the presentation would raise eyebrows and concerns among a predominantly factual audience—they will expect you to demonstrate a tried and test process that will deliver the results you had previously demonstrated. An audience with a bias toward Visionary will want to be guided toward the *Act* phase but don't make the mistake of pushing too hard—they want to get there at their own pace so a non pushy "Over to you" is preferable to a highly structured Call To Action.

Different strokes for different folks.

As this entire section has highlighted, getting a strong grasp of your audience's profile and interest is the first and most important step toward building a powerful presentation. It is the base matter upon which the remaining elements that comprise the full Presentation Lab formula sit. If you fail to invest sufficient time and energy in getting this right, the entire presentation is on shaky ground from the get-go.

With that in mind, let's now move on to the other elements that work together to create a truly powerful presentation. The next step: working to deliver your message with real clarity and power.

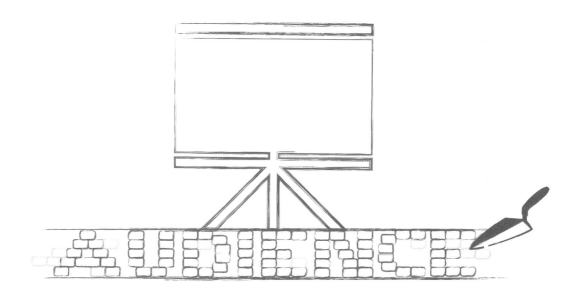

Message:
What's the Point?

C₅

Element   A B **C** D E F G H

Ev ery presentation ultimately needs to have a purpose. I considered calling this chapter "Setting Objectives" but shied away from it for the obvious reason: It makes it sound *really* boring.

And perhaps this is the reason that people typically launch into presentations with little or no thought as to their reason for being. It's remarkable how seldom business people bother to even set objectives before creating their presentation.

The truth is that you must intimately understand *why* you're presenting in order to ensure your message is robust enough. It is critical, because it is the framework upon which you build the content and visuals of your presentation.

The good news is that we don't subscribe to the drawn out process of creating totally SMART (specific, measurable, attainable, relevant and time-bound) objectives for *most* presentations. Like you, we're keen to get started on building the presentation. But we do need to make sure we lay the right foundations before diving in.

We use a much simpler brainstorming process called **Must-Intend-Like** to get a firm grip on the objectives for any presentation. The great news is that you can use this approach for all manner of things—from setting the objectives for important phone calls to agreeing where the next family holiday will be. It's powerful stuff.

In short, this is an area you simply cannot afford to skip over...

Step 1

Using whatever method feels most natural to you (whiteboard, mindmap, Word document, back of an envelope, etc.), think through and jot down a few key considerations for the upcoming presentation:

- Who will be there?

- How long do you have with them?

- How long has this been on your schedule?

  o Is it a recent development, or has this been planned for some time?

- Why are they seeing you?

  o What do you believe they are looking to achieve from the presentation?

Don't worry; you're not looking to write *War and Peace* here. You just need enough to get your thoughts straight, and start thinking about the possibilities the presentation holds.

Step 2

Next, you'll create a separate list; but this time, it is all about **you**:

- What are the fundamental reasons you are presenting?

  o Is it to make a sale?

  o Share an idea you want your audience to support?

  o Report on progress?

- Why are **you** personally presenting?

  o Your knowledge and experience?

  o Your position or profile within the business?

- What history do you have with the audience?

  o Do they know you and/or your company?

  o Is there a level of trust already established?

  o Is this a follow up presentation to a previous engagement (presentation, proposal, networking event)?

Step 3

Using the information you now have, take a final page and split it into three columns entitled **Must**, **Intend**, and **Like**. Revisit the observations you've already noted and start making some judgment calls on the upcoming presentation.

Must	Intend	Like

Must

These are the *minimum* results you are looking to achieve from the presentation.

For example, you might set the minimum bar for a sales presentation at something akin to "give a good impression and ensure that our reputation as a worthy partner goes unblemished." For an internal presentation, it might be something like "ensure that all parties understand the progress we have made over the last quarter and the impact it will have on the business going forward."

Always refer back to your previous notes. If you believe the audience is merely there to "kick tires" and is not serious about proceeding with a purchase in the short term, factor this in to your "Must."

Importantly, don't set the bar too low. The objectives you set here will form the basis of your presentation story, so going for too easy an option will do nothing more than limit your overall effectiveness.

 ## Intend

These are the results you are expecting to achieve based on a well-run presentation with sufficient time and the right audience in place. In a sales scenario, it might be "to build sufficient trust with the prospect to the point that they ask us to return and demo our solution;" or, for an internal audience, "request further information so that the board can present our progress to investors on the next call."

Again, be realistic. If your initial thoughts indicate that the audience is conservative, or that your time with them is shorter than you would have ideally liked, factor that in when setting objectives.

Like

This is when you get the opportunity to be a little more optimistic and set yourself some stretch targets. Working out your "Like" can be quite a personal thing and may not be commercially driven, but it can be a huge motivator and driver when pulling together the content of your presentation.

Sales examples might be "at their request, move immediately to the demo stage." An internal meeting option might be, "that the CEO asks you to spend some time one-to-one sharing your vision for the project."

Setting strong and realistic objectives is absolutely essential to having a strong presentation message; the two are symbiotic. The Must-Intend-Like process ensures that you set yourself realistic targets and that, as you build your presentation, you don't forget the reason(s) you're doing it.

With these in mind, we'll move on to **message creation**.

Presentation Controls

Must

Intend

Like

Messaging:
Simplicity Is Not Stupidity

C₆

Element   A B **C** D E F G H

I'm all for simplicity in messaging. There's plenty of opportunity and space in your presentation's content to show your audience how clever you are if you so wish. But simplicity should always rule in messaging.

And the reason is simple: Simplicity works.

However, *simple* doesn't mean "dumbed down"; far from it. Keeping things simple while retaining meaning is actually quite tricky. And in these days of powerful presentation slideware, a gazillion technology channels, and limited time, it's easy to make things more complex than is good, or even necessary, for you or your audience.

Getting to simple takes time and a vast amount of consideration; it's the equivalent of asking an artist to create a picture using only three paints and four strokes of the paintbrush. Before even picking up the canvas, the considerate artist would take time to plan, evaluate, and test themselves and their theory fully. The same applies when creating a new presentation: Your message's clarity and simplicity needs to be the result of intense thought, debate, and review. Only once you have this in the bag can you commit yourself to creating the presentation. And although it's a huge task for any presenter, it's one to which they rarely give due consideration.

Your message needs to be simple enough for people to not only understand it quickly and fully but also to be able to *share it with others* without faltering.

In addition to the Must-Intend-Like process, a useful test for me when working with customers is to ponder if my young daughter would understand it. The project might be to launch a new bit of clever technology that comes with all manner of whizzy elements and reference the latest and greatest new information technology (IT) trends; but the *message* needs to make sense to an eight-year-old. Otherwise, it won't work.

If we can boil the message down to a simple, "*it saves the company money and keeps customers happy because it's quicker and doesn't break down,*" we're onto a winner. If the message is a little more complex (and in IT, they usually are), "*it addresses the growing redundancy issue of the mainframe ecosystem whilst embracing big data,*" I know my daughter would quickly turn around and return to the important task of organizing her plastic monster collection.

Yes, it's blindingly obvious. But members of the corporate world have a funny way of taking the straightforward and making it complex so that it sounds a little more grown up. They might do so based on the assumption that complex things sound more impressive, and they can charge more for them.

Or it might just be that people have forgotten about the basics. Either way, spending time to boil the material down to its simplest points is a surefire way to ensure that your audience leaves with your intended message, versus some smorgasbord of assumptions and guesswork.

SIMPLICITY IS NOT STUPIDITY SIMPLICITY IS NOT STUPIDITY
SIMPLICITY IS NOT STUPIDITY SIMPLICITY IS NOT STUPIDITY
SIMPLICITY IS NOT STUPIDITY SIMPLICITY IS NOT STUPIDITY
SIMPLICITY IS NOT STUPIDITY SIMPLICITY IS NOT STUPIDITY
SIMPLICITY IS NOT STUPIDITY SIMPLICITY IS NOT STUPIDITY
SIMPLICITY IS NOT STUPIDITY SIMPLICITY IS NOT STUPIDITY
SIMPLICITY IS NOT STUPIDITY SIMPLICITY IS NOT STUPIDITY
SIMPLICITY IS NOT STUPIDITY SIMPLICITY IS NOT STUPIDITY
SIMPLICITY IS NOT STUPIDITY SIMPLICITY IS NOT STUPID Y
SIMPLICITY IS NOT STUPIDITY SIMPLICITY IS
SIMPLICITY IS NOT STUPIDITY
SIMPLICITY IS NOT STUPIDITY
SIMPLICITY IS NOT STUPIDITY
SIMPLICITY IS NOT STUPIDITY
SIMPLICITY IS NOT STUPIDITY
SIMPLICITY IS NOT STUPIDITY
SIMPLICITY IS NOT STUPIDITY
SIMPLICITY IS NOT STUPIDITY
SIMPLICITY IS NOT STUPIDITY
SIMPLICITY IS NOT STUPIDITY
SIMPLICITY IS NOT STUPIDITY

Give Them Something They Will Remember…And Then Let It Travel

C₇

Element   A B **C** D E F G H

Ho w often have you sat through a presentation and then, when a colleague asked what it was all about afterward, struggled to explain it properly? Holding your hands up and dramatically declaring, "I have absolutely no idea!" might amuse others, but in reality, it reflects a huge waste of your time—and the presentation's massive failure to deliver.

Work that through to its logical conclusion: It means that pretty much everyone who sat through that presentation had the opportunity to take on board your message and share it with their colleagues, friends, lovers, and family pets. But because they either didn't understand or remember it, that opportunity has been lost. Great presentation messages have the propensity to sprout feet and travel through conversations, social media, gossip, and formal communications. Poor presentation messages never make it out the door.

So How Do You Ensure That Your Audience Remembers Your Message?

Many of my learned peers have written extensively about giving audiences that "special moment" in a presentation that they will remember long after the final slide has been shown. Well documented examples of these "gob-smacking," widely talked about moments include when Steve Jobs produced the new MacBook Air out of a standard office envelope, or when his counterpart Bill Gates opened up a jar of mosquitos within the auditorium at a TED talk.

Now, I love showmanship as much as the next man. But I fear that sometimes, people are missing the point when talking about these "special moments," specifically, that it's not the *act* that's noteworthy but the *message behind it*.

If all you can remember about Steve Jobs' MacBook Air presentation is that he pulled a neat trick on stage using a laptop computer and an envelope but you didn't grasp the message he was *really* trying to communicate, then the presentation was ultimately a failure.*

Believe it or not, it's relatively simple to create a standout moment in a presentation. It could be an arresting image on a slide, use of a prop or an exercise that involves audience members. (I've forgotten how many times I've seen a bottle of Coke and a tube of Mentos used as a tortured metaphor for a range of business topics.) It doesn't really matter what the moment is unless it helps deliver your message loud and clear. But if it doesn't support your message, it's at best redundant showmanship—and at worst a distraction that ultimately damages your presentation.

Using tricks and novelties to grab your audiences' attention is hokey. If your message is suitably powerful, you can step away from the Coke/Mentos floorshow and start to really communicate with your audience.

Much has been written about the concept and value of "hammocking" in presentations. In my humble opinion, most of this is pure bunkum, designed to disguise a poorly planned, audience agnostic, and frankly, boring presentation.

The idea is simple: Give the audience a few wake-up calls at various stages throughout the presentation to keep them engaged. These might take the form of a video clip, an audience question, or a controversial statement—anything to momentarily pull the audience back from the edge of slumber, as the graphic below depicts.

The need to use tricks to keep your audience engaged should be the first sign that things have gone awry with your presentation. What's even more of a concern is the fact that these so-called special moments may well lead your audience to remember the trick and not your presentation message. And that's nothing short of a disaster.

*I'm aware that calling Steve Jobs' messianic position as a brilliant presenter into question is verging on the sacrilegious. But what the heck; we're here to challenge the norm—because the norm is not working for most presentations.

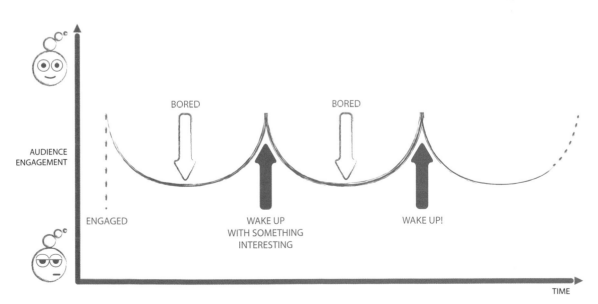

AUDIENCE ENGAGEMENT

BORED

BORED

ENGAGED

WAKE UP WITH SOMETHING INTERESTING

WAKE UP!

TIME

Don't raise your voice,
improve your argument.

Desmond Tutu

Focus on the Message First—Not the Delivery

In the end, your underlying message is what needs to live on after the presentation. If you struggle to answer a colleague's innocent "What was the presentation about?' question, the lack of clarity, focus, and simplicity around the message is likely to blame. You've got some work to do.

When we take customers through our Presentation Optimization process, we work damned hard at developing, clarifying, and testing key messages. It's important to put the time in here. After all, you want your message to continue making an impact well after you finish presenting your carefully delivered speech or beautifully designed slides.

To ensure that the messages are focused, clear, and engaging, we limit them to an absolute maximum of three points (while always striving to one killer message). We use the following questions as our litmus test:

- If I called a member of your audience two weeks after your presentation, what do you think they would remember about your presentation?

- What would you *want them* to remember about your presentation?

- Do the two currently match?

If the response from the audience member is positive but along the lines of "*I remember your beautifully designed slides*," we've failed. If, however, they respond by saying, "*Oh yes, you're the guys that can make an impact on X, Y and Z*," we've delivered a presentation with a message that has truly sprouted feet and started to spread.

Focused Messages Take Time

In many ways, a thorough understanding of audience and message seem to have been the biggest victims from today's manic and technological business world.

When the clock is ticking and you're up against a deadline, it's all too easy to make assumptions about audience stereotypes ("They're from finance so we need lots of charts") and message (selling product features over business benefits). Communication 24/7 via e-mail, phone, text, and Skype means that everyone is able to (and normally does) offer an opinion on *everything*—from presentation content and aesthetics, to which technology to employ. Presentation development by committee is fast becoming the norm—and is something technology providers are, unsuspectingly, aiding in by building collaboration functionality into their software.

Unfortunately, the net result is confused noise rather than clear messaging focused on a well-defined audience profile. You, your audience, and your presentation all deserve better than that.

Ha ving a powerful message to share is great, but it's merely the starting point of a more involved process.

Your carefully constructed and considered message needs to evolve into the basis of a story. As discussed earlier, a thoroughly developed story has the power to make your message "sticky," without having to rely on wow moments to keep your audience engaged. By introducing a structure, story, or narrative arc, you can give your message the opportunity to grow legs, travel, and get shared time and time again.

We use a process called **storyflow development** to achieve this for our customers. The concept of the storyflow took some time to come into fruition within Eyeful. Our presentation consultant team spent many years working with customers to identify their key messages.

Once confirmed, we'd dive straight into figuring out which content helped them deliver this to their audience. However, this led to a few headaches. Some customers freaked out when we started to hack away at their beloved content armed with little more than a whiteboard/flipchart full of workshop generated hieroglyphics and a confident air about ourselves. In particular, it proved difficult for our contacts to share the new Presentation Optimization–created message with their peers and superiors at this very early stage.

Yes, they could describe the new pared down message, but there was some confusion letting them know precisely how we were going to actually share it. And, "Well, you'll just have to wait and see," didn't seem to cut it.

How to Build Your Storyflow Document

The easiest way to describe the storyflow document is that it's the chapter headings of your presentation story; it highlights the structural elements, the high-level messages and the story's logical flow.

It will also highlight that points you use to jump off into more detailed sections (we'll cover the power of interactive presentations later on; as demonstrated in the graphic below, these need to be carefully planned from the very start) and also provide some rudimentary pointers in terms of script.

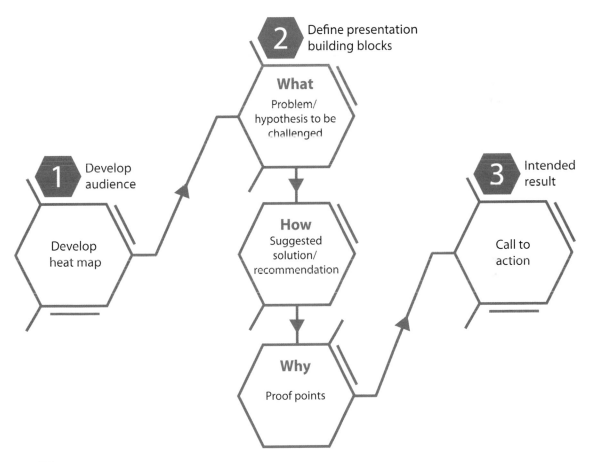

2 Define presentation building blocks

What
Problem/ hypothesis to be challenged

1 Develop audience

Develop heat map

How
Suggested solution/ recommendation

3 Intended result

Call to action

Why
Proof points

4 Develop into audience pathway structure

5 Highlight interaction/visual considerations

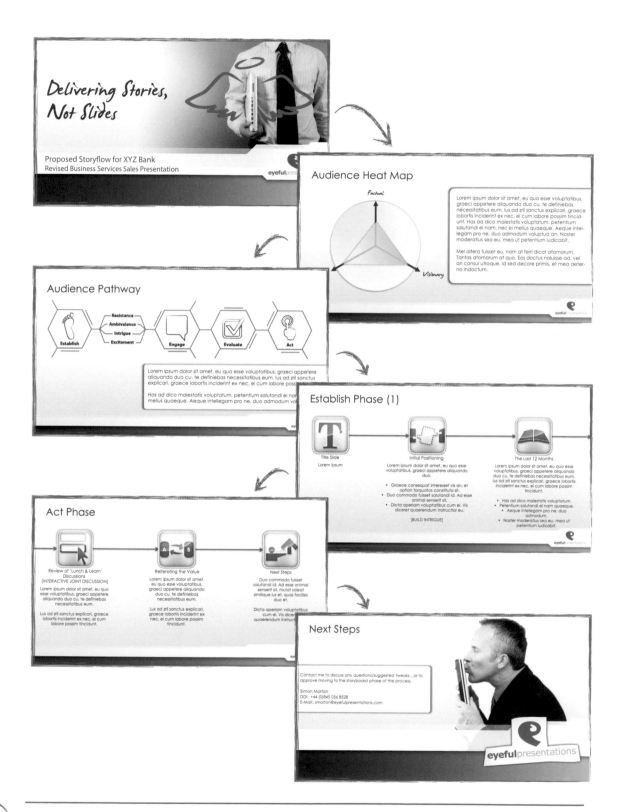

Nothing about the storyflow document is cast in stone; there should always be debate and challenge to the approach. The example opposite is a case in point. Our customer was a large retail bank who required a new approach to their sales messaging. Following a fruitful but occasionally tense workshop, we put forward a plan that to some of the more Factual personalities in the room was going to be contentious. The purpose of the storyflow was to ensure that all parties were able to view the proposed approach without the distraction or complication of detail. Once we had approval on the overarching message and structure of the story, we were able to move on to the detail as a group jointly happy with the presentation approach.

The storyflow allowed for an additional benefit: We were able to use it to keep us on the straight and narrow further down the road of presentation development. Despite the fact that we build presentations for a living—for companies of all different sizes and shapes—we're still human. And we need to ensure that the tail is not wagging the dog in terms of content and visuals. It's all too easy to get over excited when you start pulling together relevant and powerful content and developing the accompanying visuals. The storyflow document helps address that.

The good news for those of you who are desperate to begin developing your content and visuals is that once you've completed the storyflow document, we're ready to launch into the next phase of presentation development: finessing and developing your raw materials.

Shall we begin?

Creating Compelling Content

D

Element   A B C **D** E F G H

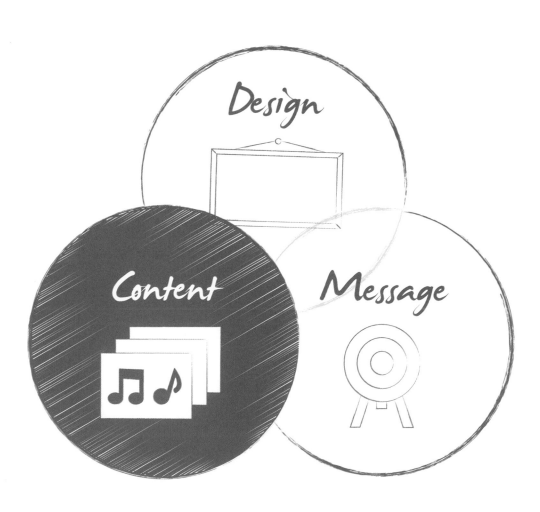

It might seem like a simple question, but it's very easy to get the wrong end of the stick. Content to many people is the information you place onto a PowerPoint slide (normally in bullet point form!) to get your message across.

But it actually goes deeper than that.

Content is the information you need your audience to **know** to help drive the message forward.

This means that, dependent on your audience, there are likely to be large chunks of content cluttering up your slide that the audience either doesn't need to know—or, more likely, is already completely au fait with and doesn't need you to remind them of.

It's useful to see content as the logical building blocks of your presentation. If you don't share salient content in a structured way, you'll never get to your goal of a completely understood, engaging and remembered message. As such, it's also a great way of building empathy and rapport with your audience by ensuring that the content you use addresses their questions, concerns and needs. Content that engages them and takes them on a personal journey is a lot more valuable and compelling than sharing fact after fact about your business and how impressive it's growth has been.

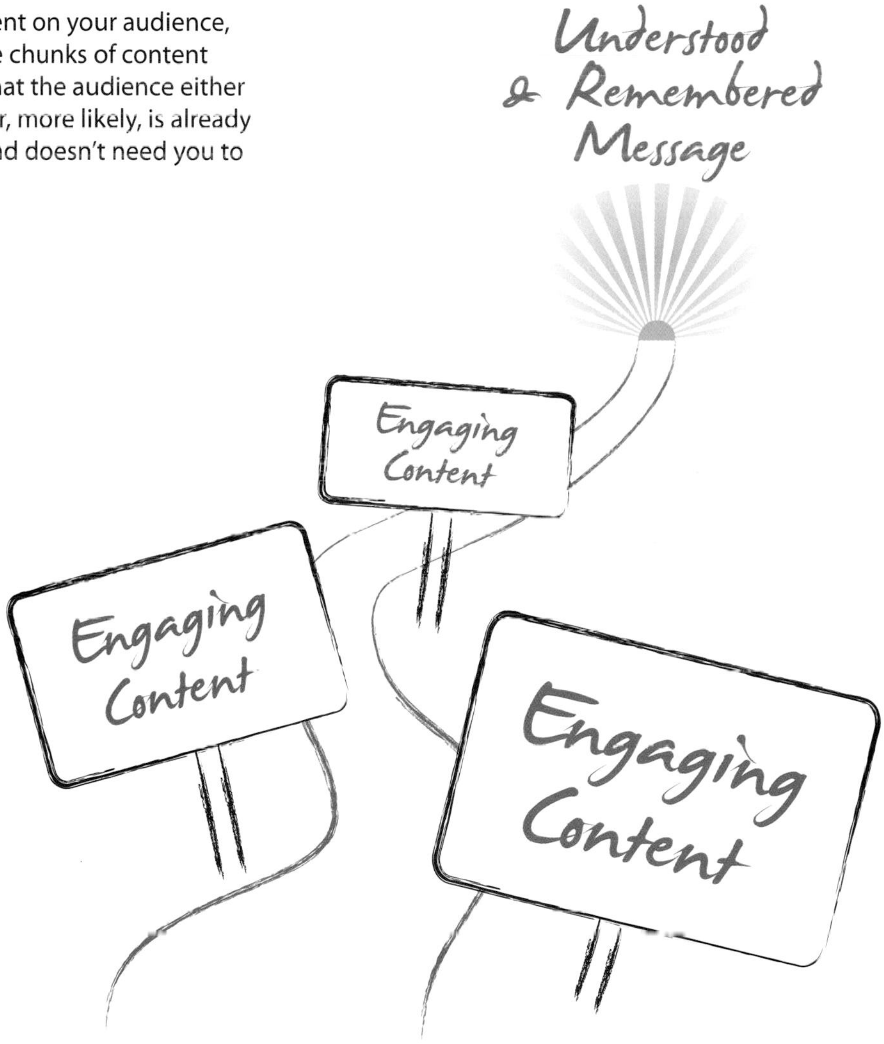

Understood & Remembered Message

Engaging Content

Engaging Content

Engaging Content

The Curse of the Credentials Presentation

Ask a business-to-business (B2B) salesperson to name their most used sales tool and they are likely to pat their laptop proudly and utter the words, "Our creds PowerPoint deck."

For the record, this tends to send shivers down my spine. This infamous and usually monstrous file is often a living example of all that is bad about corporate presentations. Let the record *also* state that this is not the fault of anyone in particular; the original deck is likely to be the lovechild of the product team, the marketing team and, at a push, the sales team. Each will have gone into this with the very best intentions:

The **Product** team wanted to ensure that all the latest specifications for the product were present, from the running speed to the size of the processor—and much more.

Marketing wanted to ensure that the deck was on brand, that it introduced the company in such a way that no one could sue for misrepresentation, and that the competition couldn't learn too much about them should the deck fall into their hands.

And **Sales** wanted to ensure the deck made them stand out from the competition. So they added cool animations, some humor, and extra text, allowing any new sales rep to grab hold of the presentation and hit the ground running.

Not a recipe for success—and, what's more, that's just the start of it. You see, those who use the deck at the "coalface" (i.e., the sales team) have likely made further embellishments over time. They will have created a few extra slides to help explain some of the more complex or esoteric parts of their proposition; they may have swapped out the template for a cool new one they downloaded from the internet or saw used at last year's company conference; and, heaven forbid (but almost guaranteed), they'll have added their own images and clipart—including holiday snaps of them on the beach by way of introduction.

All of these are major crimes and have a hugely detrimental effect on the overall quality of the presentation. But perhaps more than that, they add more and more *valueless* content to an already busy presentation. It's valueless because the vast majority of this content—both the original and the recently added—will have little or nothing to do with the audience's needs. It's more of the same "me, me, me" content that makes creds PowerPoint decks the epitome of presentation information overload.

If any of this rings a bell . . . keep reading!

The Presentation

So What Content Do I Choose?

The problem with presentation content is normally a nice one to have: There's simply too much of the stuff!

It's very rare that we come across a situation where the presenter is struggling to source sufficient content, despite this being one of their biggest fears at the start of the process. As they embark on the process of creating a presentation, they normally use the Frankenstein approach as a first option. That is, they pull together all manner of facts, visuals, and odds and ends, and then try to arrange them in such a way that begets *some* semblance of order and process.

And although it seems a natural place to start, it's often the reason for complete failure later on in the presentation process, for a few simple reasons:

- The content is rarely pulled together to support the objectives (Must-Intend-Like) and overarching message. You simply end up with a patchwork quilt of *relatively* useful content, but there's rarely a cohesive message across the entire story.

- You're likely to be sharing information that the audience is already completely in control of. This runs the risk of being boring or, even worse, coming across as condescending to the most important people in the room—your audience.

- This lack of content focus makes it very difficult to agree on what you should and shouldn't leave out—and how it all links together. Typically, most people opt for "the safe approach" and leave it all in—just in case.

This issue affects the vast majority of presenters, but as a rule, the groups that suffer most are those from an academic or scientific background, product managers, or what we fondly call the OSMCs.*

Ultimately, the compelling content should not be judged on volume. It's value lies in how much it supports and contributes to the one thing you are looking for the audience to remember—your message.

*Let me explain a little more about the curse of the OSMC, or "Old School Management Consultant." Now pretty much a footnote in business history, OSMCs had a very distinct presentation style: They specialized in confusing charts, thick reports, and interacting with a slightly supercilious air. One of the reasons for this poor state of affairs is that OSMCs were judged on the amount of data they produced. The thinking was clear—more data shared, the more comprehensive the study, and ultimately the more valuable for the client.

Unfortunately, we can still feel the OSMCs' influence across businesses today, as aspiring business leaders took their cue from this inefficient and patronizing presentation style. To make matters worse, many OSMCs made the leap from running big-ticket projects to running entire companies—making cluttered, overly complex slides the cultural norm in many corporations across the world.

Creating Compelling Content

PRESENTATIONSTEIN!!!

Additions to the product range from Trev

Updated organization charts from Jodi

New brand slides from Marketing

New contact information

Revised template slides from Hayley

European branch capability slides

Putting It to Music

Strange though it may sound, we often reference music when looking at content. Beautiful music works in a magical way by adjusting tempo, sometimes being dramatic, sometimes being subtle and gentle. For there to be a real (and ideally, emotional) connection with an audience, a presentation needs to follow much the same way.

As great jazz pioneer Charles Mingus once said . . .

I love this quote so much that I have a huge poster in my office so as to constantly remind me of the importance of simplicity in terms of content. I've also lost count of the number of times I've sent pictures of it to customers as a gentle (but not so subtle!) reminder to cut back on the content and only leave in the good stuff.

I'm a huge music fan but am one of those frustrating sorts who like a bit of everything— jazz, rock, funk, even a little folk now and then. Each genre brings with it different tempos, different attitudes, and, I can assure you having been to a fair few gigs, very different audiences (the piercings per person ratio goes off the scale at folk events).

Yet despite all these differences, there are also a vast number of similarities. They all have the same chords and musical notes to work with as their foundation and typically their heartfelt lyrics cover many of the same topics:

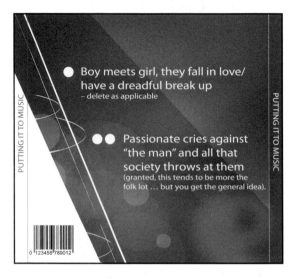

Um . . . that tends to be it.

No matter what the genre, one of the other key similarities among the top-notch composers out there is their understanding of the art of the song. Great musicians know *all* the notes and chords, of course, yet they choose to use them sparingly and to maximum effect. It's easy to spot those who might possess all the required technical prowess on their chosen instrument but has little musicianship; they're the ones who try and cram as many notes and fancy chords into every bar of music.

I personally don't have a musical bone in my body. However, I have sufficient knowledge to know that you don't play a sad song in a major key or a happy song in a minor key. But it's more than that—it's about knowing which notes to play (and not to play) to help you get your message across.

Great melodic, emotional, and resonating music relies as much on the notes that you *don't* play as the notes that make it into your song. The pauses, the rhythm, the *soul* of music comes from the composer's ability to carefully choose which notes add to their message and which ones don't.

All of the above applies equally to presentation content. As **presentation "composers,"** we face the same challenges and choices. We need to use only the most relevant and powerful content, use it at the right times, and with the right aims in mind (which, yep, are all about supporting the message, but you knew that).

THE PRESENTATION LAB

Slicing Up Your Content (With a Little Help from Occam's Razor)

D₂

> *Everything should be made as simple as possible, but not simpler.*

Quote attributed to **Albert Einstein**

Co ntent represents one of the biggest challenges the business presenter faces: It's a scarily fragile balance to maintain.

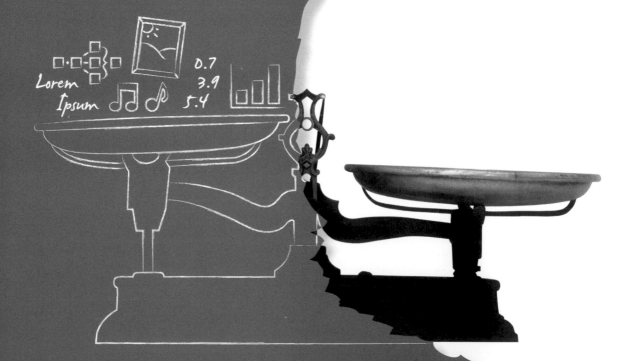

On one side, if you encumber your presentation with too much content it will become immobile. It's as if the presentation becomes overweight and flabby; it runs short of breath and slowly grinds to a halt.

On the other side, if your presentation is too light on content, your entire message is fundamentally built on sand. It's flaky, it's fragile, and it leaves your message wide open to audience skepticism.

It all comes down to the art of editing (or, more likely, self-editing in presentations). It's an art form rarely given the credit it deserves. For example, the editor's impact is too often overlooked in film and TV. (Can you name anyone who's won an Oscar for editing? Nope, me neither.)

Film editors are often seen as nothing more than a technical support act to the director, screenwriters, and actors. Yet it is their sense of what should stay in the picture and what should be left as a remnant on the cutting room floor that can make all the difference. As with presentations, editing is all about maintaining the fragile balance between sufficient content and clutter. Film editor Walter Murch describes the role perfectly: "A cross between a short-order cook and a brain surgeon" (Source: National Public Radio).

Editing is tricky . . . very tricky. So how can you ensure that you've got the balance right? By far the easiest first step is to ask yourself one simple question:

What information do I need to share with my audience to ensure that they have sufficient background to engage with my message?

Make no bones about it—the primary purpose of content within your presentation is to *support your message*. Verbose flabby presentations tend to be full of content that is, at best, simply superfluous—and at worst, full of "noise" meant to mask the presenter's lack of clarity or knowledge. You'll recall from your school days that it was always easier to pad an essay on a topic that you didn't know a huge amount about than to create a succinct and focused essay on something you *did* understand. Presentations tend to fall into the same trap.

So how do you cut to the chase and build a presentation on those prime cuts of content? The good news is that you are not the only person tasked with deciding what key information to share. Scholars, scientists, and speechwriters all struggle with the question of what to leave in and what to dispose of. Our answer borrows heavily from a theoretical approach known as Occam's razor, which provides a simple guide to getting to the core of an issue.

The thinking is pretty straight forward—when there are two explanations for the same thing, the **simpler** of the two explanations is likely to be the **correct** one.

From a scientific standpoint, this means that delving into hugely detailed possibilities and flights of fancy will, more often than not, lead you down some dead ends. On the other hand, sticking with the basic information available to you will typically lead you to the correct conclusion.

And so it goes with presentation content. Keep it as simple, clear, and uncluttered as possible to get to your intended conclusion. Not only will unnecessary material hinder your audience's engagement with the topic in hand, it could also send you down some blind alleys.

Stephen Hawking, a chap who knows a fair bit about communicating very complex matters in an engaging way, mentions Occam's razor in his masterpiece, *A Brief History of Time*:

```
"We could still imagine that there is a set of laws that
determines events completely for some supernatural being,
who could observe the present state of the universe
without disturbing it.  However, such models of the
universe are not of much interest to us mortals.  It seems
better to employ the principle known as Occam's razor
and cut out all the features of the theory that cannot
be observed."
```

This approach supports the Presentation Lab mantra of "simplicity is not stupidity." That is, by working with the most important and relevant elements of your content, you are able to deliver a quick and engaging explanation to support your message. Each type of audience profile, from the factual to the visionary, needs this content foundation upon which to build their own opinions. If this foundation becomes overcomplicated or fragile due to tenuous links or too much hypothesizing, you and your message could be in trouble.

Applying an Occam's razor approach to your presentations can take time and practice. As business presenters, it is all too easy to become overly connected with the content that you have spent hours, days, weeks, or months pulling together. The process of culling large elements can test the most hard-hearted of us!

All of this said, the concept of Occam's razor is not without it's detractors.

The Internet continues to bubble away with debate regarding Albert Einstein's use of Occam's razor when trying to define and explain fluctuations in "space-time" (worry not—this won't be on the exam and I won't waste your time or mine trying to explain quite how space-time was fluctuating and why we should be interested in the first place).

Einstein stuck with a (comparatively) straightforward approach based on his theory of relativity—one that allowed him to define his theory in terms of a rather natty equation. Although still very much a head-scratcher for the likes of me, it's based on known elements used within a defined equation that people in this field would grasp more easily.

On the other hand, Einstein's rival Hendrik Lorentz was pursuing his own theory around space-time and had concluded that the fluctuations were caused by motion through the "ether". The concept of ether was simply too complicated and theoretical for people to really take on board, so, slowly but surely, the support of influential academics and physicists fell to Einstein.

The "simple is beautiful" approach that underpins Occam's razor won again. Who knows—had it not been for Occam's razor, Warhol pictures of Hendrik Lorentz may well adorn the walls of student bedrooms across the world instead of Einstein. It's a powerful tool.

The Presentation Lab Razor—Preparation

With an eye firmly on the theory (and skepticism!) of Occam's razor, we've developed different approaches for ridding your presentation of content clutter, either when creating one from scratch or enhancing/developing an existing deck.

Both scenarios require that we observe some basic content editing rules, courtesy of our old friend The Eight Cognitive Communication Principles—three of which really come into play.

As before, lay out all of your content on a large flat surface (table, desk, floor) and go and grab a coffee. It's important to disconnect yourself from the content you've worked so hard to pull together.

Once the coffee has reached sipping temperature, return to your content and start applying the following recognized psychological considerations:

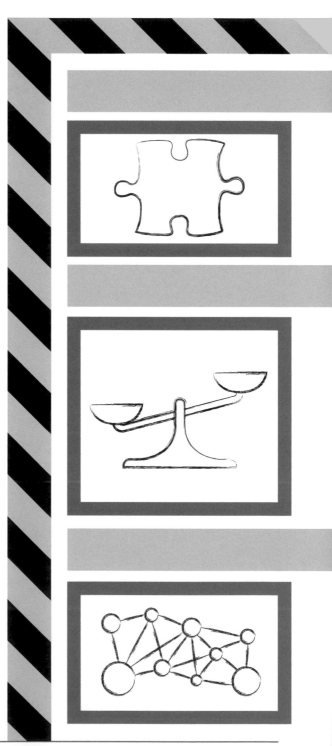

Compatibility

Compatibility is about ensuring that all the presentation elements work as if they belong together, be that from a content perspective or in terms of visual branding. As soon as you leave an incompatible bit of content in your presentation, it will stick out like the proverbial sore thumb, distracting your audience and generally serving no purpose.

Relevance

Closely aligned to Compatibility is **Relevance**. Best described as "not being able to see the forest for the trees," relevance focuses on the human brain's extraordinary automatic problem-solving capabilities.

If there's too little content in place, your audience will look to fill in the gaps through assumptions. This brings with it the inevitable risk of them reaching the incorrect conclusions and threatening your message's power and impact. Equally, provide too much content and your audience will jump straight into filtering mode, which carries equals risks of them grabbing hold of the wrong end of the stick.

The answer to the conundrum is obvious: Only use content that is completely relevant and supports your key message.

Discriminability

Finally, we have **Discriminability**. This is a fancy way of describing the most basic of presentation rules. Big blocks of information on a slide do very little to help your audience engage with you and your message.

Bombarding your audience with content, no matter how relevant and supportive, does little more than overload them with information and ultimately lose their attention. The audience needs your assistance to Discriminate the information you're feeding them and digest it in the right order and at the right time.

The Presentation Lab Razor—Define & Declutter

With the basics in place, you are now in a position to start working your way through the process of defining and decluttering your content so only the strongest and most relevant survives.

Option 1
A Sparkling Brand New Presentation

The first and easiest approach is to start your presentation from scratch. By going through the process of understanding your audience, fine-tuning your message, and creating a bespoke storyflow document, you're well on your way.

The storyflow document does a wonderful job at signposting what content should and shouldn't be included in your final presentation. By creating the story up front, you will have self-edited much of the superfluous information out of the structure, knowing that any unnecessary diversions will only impede your message's effectiveness.

With this in mind, simply choose the content that is **really necessary** for your audience to engage with and understand in line with your storyflow document. Everything else left on the cutting room floor is unnecessary.

Option 2
Optimizing an Existing Presentation

Although it would be wonderful to think that you'll develop *all* presentations from scratch, the reality is most are either carbon copies of earlier pitches/speeches or an untidy smorgasbord of different slides and ideas from an array of sources. Although I'd implore you to start from a blank piece of paper (à la the full Presentation Optimization process), I also recognize that real life occasionally gets in the way—and you may need to pull together a presentation in a very limited time. So here goes.

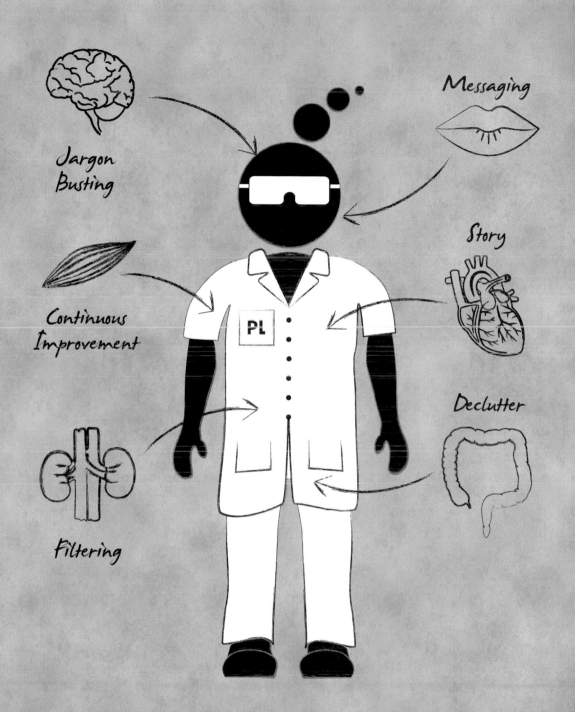

Jargon Busting

Messaging

Continuous Improvement

Story

Filtering

Declutter

PL

Stage 1
Messaging

Simply because you are working from an existing deck (or collection of decks) does not get you off the hook when it comes to reaffirming your message. By taking the time to either establish or reengage with the message, you are giving yourself the very best chance of keeping the best content and ditching the excess.

Stage 2
Story

Again, you may believe that the story is already in place when using an existing presentation. However, taking time to review and tweak it accordingly will give you the confidence to deliver a more succinct presentation.

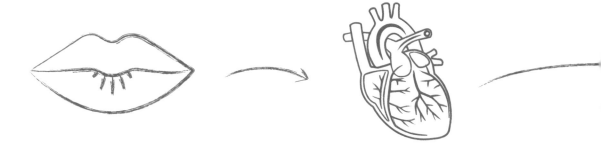

Consider your new audience and their Factual/Emotional/Visionary heat map profile. What will they be taking away from your message that you might not have previously considered? What are their Musts, Intends, and Likes?

Think about how the story will resonate with the different audience profiles (Factual, Emotional, and Visionary) and ensure that you have these elements straight in your own mind. Once these aims are compiled, you are able to move to the next phase—applying the correct content to help support your story.

Creating Compelling Content

Stage 3
Filtering

This is the relatively simple process of identifying which elements of your plentiful content will assist your audience in understanding and moving through each of the chapters of your story. Again, a good understanding of your audience's profile will help here. How much Factual content to do you need to bring to the table versus Emotional or Visionary?

Stage 4
Jargon Busting

Jargon is a peculiar phenomenon. It can seem to appear out of the ether and settle into presentations without business presenters ever really noticing. It's only after a few less-than-stellar presentation performances that presenters review their decks and realize that their slides, their notes and their script are full of TLAs (three-letter acronyms, to you and me).

Filter out the information that doesn't serve this purpose. For example, demonstrating that you've worked really hard and know a lot about your subject might make *you* feel better, but it's unlikely to have a huge impact on the final decision made by an external procurement team. Leave in the content that matters to them; you can use everything else in the hard copy handout later.

Business jargon has now reached epidemic proportions. People no longer find it a sign of subject matter expertise or greater intelligence; they find it tiresome. There is also the very real risk that your audience could feel intimidated by their inability to decipher your TLA and jargon-heavy presentation. They disengage with you and your message more quickly and remind you of a crucial presentation rule: as the presenter, it is incumbent on *you* to keep the audience comfortable and engaged with the content. If they can't keep up, the fault lies with the way you've positioned the material—not with their inability to grasp it.

If you fear that you are have "gone native" and can no longer distinguish between jargon and normal speech (it happens to us all), call on a friend outside of your industry or business to sense check things. You may be surprised at how much jargon has worked it's way into your vocabulary!

So much technical gobbledygook is spewed out in various forms that the United Kingdom now has a central body called the Plain English Campaign to identify culprits and reward plain-speaking direct communicators.

So me people think that flowery language and complicated writing is a sign of intellectual strength. They are wrong. Some of our greatest communicators were—and are—passionate believers in the simplicity of the written word. As Winston Churchill described a particularly tortured piece of officialese: "This is the sort of English up with which I will not put."

Baroness Thatcher, former Prime Minister, in a letter to the Plain English Campaign

The good news is that by ridding your presentation of jargon and gobbledygook, you kill two birds with one stone: You declutter the content, **and** you further increase the chances of your audience understanding what you're talking about.

Stage 5
Declutter

By this stage, you should be in a very comfortable position. All the content you have left provides value and is ordered in a way that supports your key message. You've stripped out all the unnecessary "corporate twaddle" that can slowly kill the audience's engagement and thus your key message.

But there's still more you can do.

Stage 6
Continuous Improvement

Short term—Go to Stage 4 and repeat before every meeting.

Longer term—Go to Stage 1 and repeat at least once every 6 months.

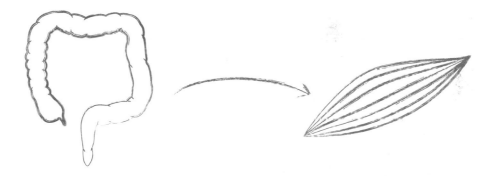

At this stage, it's all about the fine-tuning of your content. You should be looking to remove the superfluous words (ditching adjectives and verbs is relatively easy if you're delivering the presentation "live") and conveying the information in tables and data as visuals or charts.

Fundamentally, getting content right is about keeping it relevant, structured, and as simple as possible; it's no more complex than that. With this in mind, we need to turn our attentions to the process of bringing the message and content to life through Valuable Visuals.

It would seem that there are certain rules and regulations that have become almost acceptable to disobey.

For instance, the motorway speed limit is 70 mph in the United Kingdom. Yet for the life of me, I can't remember the last time I saw anyone drive at less than 80 mph on a clear carriageway—despite the fact that all drivers are fully aware that the speed limit is there to protect them and their passengers in case of an accident.

Another example would be the age at which young adults partake of their first alcoholic beverage. Of course, the law states one thing, but society on the whole accepts that it will happen earlier. And as long as all involved are safe, no one gets into trouble. The law exists to protect our young people's health and wellbeing—yet many people happily turn a blind eye.

Most pertinently to the Presentation Lab, businesspeople know that creating text heavy slides is simply not the way to do things. It breaks the most basic rules of presentations that they fully recognize and understand. They'll happily acknowledge that too much text kills any opportunity to engage their audience and makes them less likely to meet their objectives. They're well aware doing so reinforces the generally held belief that all business presentations, well, suck.

Yet they still do it . . . time and time again.

It's really quite remarkable behavior from otherwise rational and professional business people, especially when they know that they are the root cause of the issue.

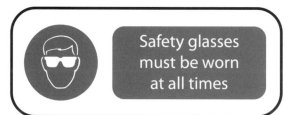

So as we move on to creating the visual tools to support your presentation message and share your content, it's time to make a few assumptions.

That you, the learned reader of this book, already know that too much text and distracting wacky animations on a slide is bad and that powerful visuals are good.

That you know how to add visuals to your slideware of choice, whether it's PowerPoint, Keynote, or whichever flavor-of-the-month tool is being hawked around business circles at the time of reading.

That you are not equipped with a limitless budget to purchase high resolution images from picture libraries. Equally, you're not blessed with an intimate knowledge of Photoshop, Illustrator, or other image manipulation software.

With this in mind, let's focus on the impact Valuable Visuals can have on your presentation and how to ensure that you present the best option each and every time.

THE PRESENTATION LAB

A Picture Paints a Thousand (Different) Words . . .

D₄

Element   A B C **D** E F G H

Helium Nitrogen Oxygen Argon Carbon Dioxide Neon Methane
Oxygen Hydrogen
Steel Aluminium Titanium
Sulphur Hydrogen Helium Oxygen Carbon Nitrogen Silicon Magnesium Neon Iron
Sitka Spruce Picea Sitchensis
Lolium Perenne
Petroica Macrocephala Tomtit
White-tailed Deer Odocoileus virginianus
Calcium Carbonate

The Power of Visuals

I feel like I should start with an apology. Kicking off a section regarding visuals with the somewhat trite "a picture paints a thousand words" could be viewed by many as a bit of a cop-out. It's as obvious as the multitude of other rules that business presenters choose to ignore, yet when you dig a little deeper, this hackneyed phrase simply and clearly summarizes the importance of presentation visuals.

It is no exaggeration to say that the stakes rise to new heights when considering how to visualize and support your presentation message. Get your visuals right, and you're well on the way to getting your audience hooked. Get them wrong, and you could confuse or disengage them irreparably.

VISUALS

Creating Compelling Content

The Power of Visuals + Message

Well-chosen images not only help demonstrate a point but also lock it into your audience's psyche. The visual is often the key to them remembering and being able to share/act on your message; it acts as the synapse to recall.

This vital link between visuals and your message is an essential part of the Presentation Lab process. The whole is so much greater than the sum of the parts.

VISUALS   MESSAGE

Scientific Proof

Happily, the scientific evidence stacks up to support this claim. As California State University's Paul Martin Lester concluded in his study, "Syntactic Theory of Visual Communication," people generally remember 10 percent of what they hear and 20 percent of what they read.

So far, so very Albert Mehrabian (reference earlier chapter). However, things get particularly interesting when information is presented to them in a combined visual and oral format: Retention leaps to an impressive 80 percent. This is welcome news to any presenter with an important message to share.

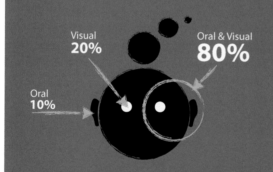

An often-quoted study by Wharton School of Business concluded that

67% of audiences felt that presenters who combined both visual and verbal elements were more persuasive—music to the ears of any sales presenter with a target to reach.

The desire to persuade underpins the majority of presentations. A prime reason for people putting themselves through the frequently scary process of presenting is to persuade their audience to follow their proposed course of action. As a result, presenters are understandably always on the look out for the element that makes all the difference and gets the audience thinking in their terms. According to Ann Marie Barry of Boston College, images combined with a strong message may well be the key:

"[It is visual communication that] sets up our cognitive thinking, skewing it automatically toward a particular response."*

*"Visual Communication Diversity," ExpertClick.

So there would seem to be no end to the power of the visual as an element of your presentation formula. The logic behind this power is pretty obvious:

- We think visually.
- We remember visually.
- We engage visually way more often than we do with other senses.

Indeed, this is one of the reasons many people close their eyes when listening or thinking intently. It's all about shutting off our predominant sense of sight.

" *My style of songwriting is influenced by cinema. I'm a frustrated filmmaker. A fan once said to me, 'Girl, you make me see pictures in my head!' and I took that as a great compliment. That's exactly my intention.* "

Joni Mitchell, Singer, Activist

For this simple reason, images in a presentation contain incredible power and as a result, need to be treated with the utmost respect. Take a moment to think about the emotions stirred by the important or powerful images in your own life. Some of these emotions are likely to come from incredibly personal images—they could be screensaver pictures of your children growing up, a old printed photograph from your wedding day album, or a polaroid of the home you grew up in. The strength of feeling you get from recalling and viewing these personal artifacts is incredibly powerful—it gets you deep inside.

But emotionally powerful images are not just reserved for emotional stimuli from your personal experiences; they can also come from your own sense of self and position within society. Take the example of a fading pop star who was so moved by the powerful imagery featured in a 1984 TV news report of the famine in Ethiopia that he started a movement that fundamentally changed the way people view charity and the world at large.

The TV pictures of Ethiopian children dying in biblical numbers sparked something in Sir Bob Geldof, then a comfortably well off but relatively unremarkable lead singer in a rock and roll band.

The passion and energy these images prompted in Sir Bob compelled him to take a series of actions—from organizing a charity single to setting up an iconic transatlantic pop concert in 1985, a time when transatlantic travel was tricky! Live Aid alone raised more than $280 million (USD) and was viewed by an estimated 400 million people across 60 countries.

An amazing feat delivered by a remarkable man but sparked by incredible visuals.

The immense power of images can prompt people to do amazing things, follow particular flights of fancy, or just start to think differently. As such, it is incumbent on us as presenters to use the right type of imagery and visuals to guide our audience through the story in support of our message.

"

The scenes were absolutely riveting. This from the get-go did not look like television—it looked like Spartacus, something vast . . . And it was grey . . . these grey raphes moving in this grey moonscape.

And the camera was pitching us . . . it was like a Cyclops, just there . . .

It would not let you off the hook.

"

Bob Geldof

Caution is advised when it comes to using certain analogies. There is a (possibly apocryphal) story of an information technology (IT) company who wanted to win the hearts and minds of their sales team as they pushed forward into a new financial year. As is often the approach in that sector, they decided to run a large sales conference in London and fly their representatives in from across the world to learn about new products, share experiences, and have their CEO, CMO, and the rest of the company's leaders "fire them up." It's a tried and trusted approach, and so they threw themselves into the project with gusto.

So far, so good.

The company was aware of the importance of a strong theme for the event. They knew they could use visuals to support the theme, maybe throw in some related video and use it as a way of tying the various speaker presentations together. In light of the tough times ahead, conference organizers agreed upon a theme of "rebirth." This would allow them to demonstrate no matter how difficult times got, no matter how hard the competition tried to grind you down and no matter how gloomy you might be feeling, there was always a way to win and come out on top. It was to be a celebration of the tenacity and bravery of the human spirit (applied to IT sales).

So far, so good.

But then things went horribly awry.

Someone, somewhere within the company decided to ditch the so often used but ultimately tired analogies of sportsmen and women fighting their way back from adversity and instead chose to use the September 11th attacks on New York as the visual metaphor for the event. They reasoned that if the people of New York and the Western world as a whole could pick themselves up from such an apocalyptic event and come back stronger than ever, anyone could.

By way of drawing a parallel to a huge personal struggle, it's beyond tasteless . . . **but** you can understand where the germ of the idea came from. There is no doubt that the way the United States and especially New Yorkers proudly battled against the horror that befell them is inspiring. It does demonstrate the strength and power of the human spirit; however, as a visual metaphor, it's simply too raw, too crass, and too visceral an event to ever attempt to use as a theme for a corporate conference.

PowerPoint slides were created with images of the devastation left in New York. Video clips were shown to set the scene at the start of the presentation. Speaker presentations were themed around the different elements of the tragedy.

Naturally, audience members were appalled at the clumsy and tasteless comparison. A few of them had lost friends and relatives in the 9/11 attacks; others knew someone who had been affected; and the remainder had felt the same sense of panic and loss when they had witnessed the news that day.

The visual metaphor had horrifically backfired and left everyone, from organizers to audience members, somewhat shell-shocked.

Impact

Retention

Sensitivity

Using visual themes is a wonderful and powerful way to get your audience on the same page. Using images effectively can spark ideas, emotion and enthusiasm within your audience. But it is imperative that you choose *the right ones*. Using shocking or provocative images might grab attention and become a talking point (often for the wrong reasons), but can ultimately create a barrier between your audience and your message. (More on that shortly.)

In short, proceed with caution.

SLOW
PROCEED WITH
CAUTION

The Super Powers of Visual Subtext

If simple visuals are a powerful way of engaging your audience and sharing your message, things go to a whole new level once you understand the importance and impact of working with a *visual subtext*.

What do we mean by visual subtext? It's probably best to demonstrate how this works by way of a simple example—like the following picture of a house:

The general subtext here is likely to be relatively far-reaching to those within your audience. It's a nice looking house surrounded by perfect blue skies and beautiful trees. But your audience's immediate response is likely to be less about the facts and more about the emotions it evokes.

It might cause some to think about their own home and the warmth and safety they feel when they are there. Others might be considering their aspirations, perhaps planning on moving or working toward owning a house of this size. It could also prompt them to imagine fun family days in the sun, perhaps playing with the kids in the garden or barbecuing with friends.

The list of emotions and feelings generated by one simple photo could go on and on. There is a risk that the presenter doesn't have *complete* control over the emotions the image stirs, but after some consideration, you get a sense of what impact this picture is likely to have on your audience. However, much more important than control at this stage is the simple fact that the audience will have *emotionally engaged* with the image. Rather than force-feeding them information, you have encouraged them to use the picture to start building a story all of their own.

As we start to add more context to the house, the opportunity for the audience to emotionally engage with the image slowly dissipates. One simple (and fairly obvious!) message suddenly drags us away from the wide-focus emotional engagement with the image and starts to take us down a particular route.

As we build more and more context (for which you can read "content"), the less we are able to reference our initial emotional response to the picture.

House set in beautiful countryside with ample parking

By the time we get to this version of the image, we're more focused on the material structure and house's layout rather than its original emotional qualities as a home. Although these contextual features may be useful to an audience made up of realtors, the emotional response that accompanied our initial response has long since disappeared into the ether.

As soon as you start adding more copy around an image, you cut down the opportunity for people to create and engage with their own subtext.

So what?

Well, we cannot dismiss the importance of letting the subtext *breathe*.

Unhindered subtext sparks strong emotions which deliver that Holy Grail for presenters—a stickier and longer-lasting message.

Managing an audience that is enjoying its own personal trip down memory lane is important. You want to emotionally stimulate people, but you need to ensure that they stay on track and engaged with your message. The trick here is to accompany your powerful visuals with other stimuli to guide the audience through the process, from the few carefully chosen words you decide to add to the slide or by the content you share vocally or by structuring and sequencing your story.

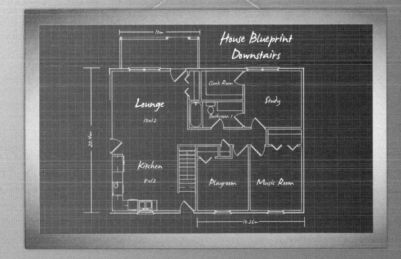

Beware of the Second Story Syndrome!

As already explained, visuals are powerful elements within a presentation. They have the ability to engage, inspire, and take your audience on a flight of fancy as soon as you reveal them.

However, you need to carefully harness this power, because uncontrolled visuals can spark off the most unexpected thoughts in your audience members, thereby allowing their minds to wander—and leaving you fighting to get them back on track.

The threat of a "second story" is most prevalent in formal presentations (reference the **Presentation Landscape** section for a full description). This is when the engagement of audience to visual elements is at it's most intense as there is little or no *direct* interaction with the presenter. They'll pick up on the smallest of things, from an innocent typo (often a sign that the presenter was still tweaking and working on their slides the night before) to use of a particular font. Your audience's visual sense is heightened, and they're looking for something to latch onto.

This is the perfect opportunity for the dreaded "second story" to rear it's ugly head.

'Second story' is the independent mental journey an audience member takes when prompted by something you say, do, or show. Something as simple as an image of a computer on a screen might launch a whole internal debate within this person's mind:

"Hmmm . . . interesting. Why did they choose an Apple laptop for that picture? Don't they trust Windows? Does their software even run on Windows? Or do they see themselves as just too cool to be seen on a normal Windows computer? Perhaps they are a little arrogant? I noticed the presenter is using a Windows PC; is this because he's low down the food chain?"

All of this internal dialogue, created from just one innocent picture of a computer!

The fact of the matter is that there is no way to avoid the "second story" syndrome. The spark of thought that comes from seeing an image for the first time plays a vital role in making the most out of visual subtext. This helps lock in your message—so make the most of this phenomenon. But be aware that it can take your audience down unintended avenues of thought.

Avenues that you may not be able to drag them back from . . .

Story Map

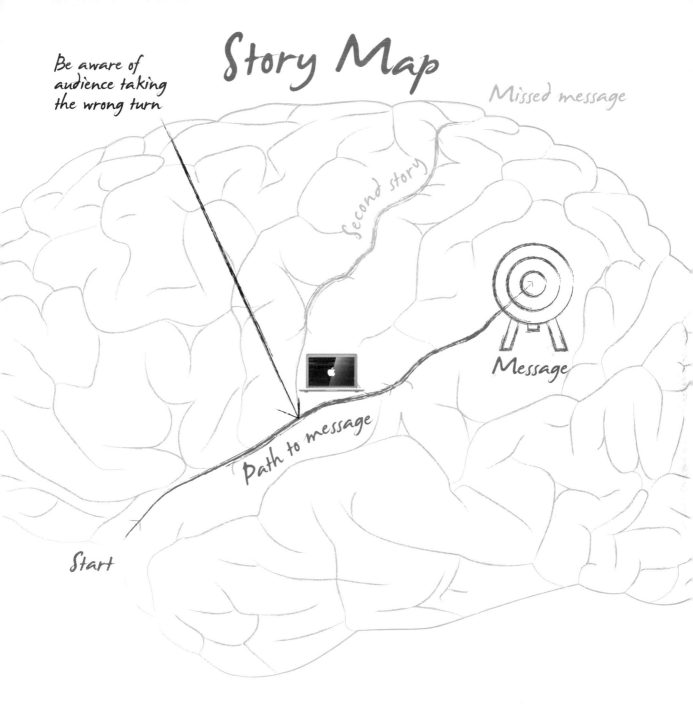

Be aware of audience taking the wrong turn

Missed message

Second story

Message

Path to message

Start

By using these techniques in conjunction with emotionally powerful images, you will be able to ensure that the audience follows you rather than you having to try to round them up every 5 minutes.

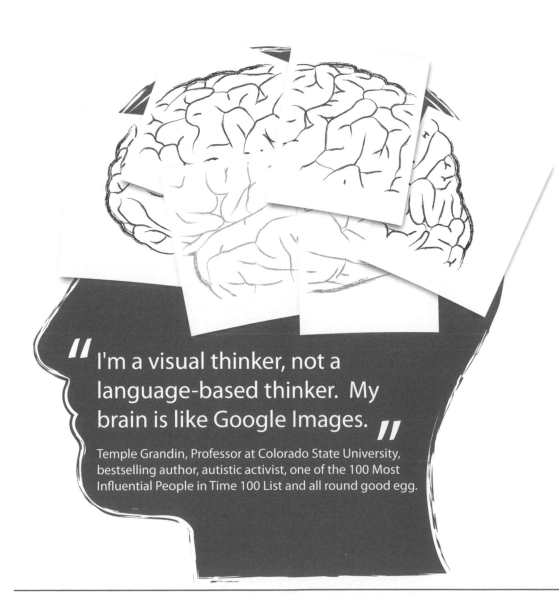

"I'm a visual thinker, not a language-based thinker. My brain is like Google Images."

Temple Grandin, Professor at Colorado State University, bestselling author, autistic activist, one of the 100 Most Influential People in Time 100 List and all round good egg.

Your audience is made up of people just like you and me. Over time, we've been spoiled (in the nicest possible way) by the incredibly fast change of technology. The old way of doing things has moved on and gotten, well, better.

Where once we had to actually attend a concert to see our favorite artists perform, we can now simply watch last night's gig on YouTube (albeit on a very shaky mobile phone shot video with a very loud and irritating audience member singing out of tune).

Where once we had to wait for the news to air on TV or radio, we now jump onto our smartphones or tablets and view live footage wherever we are.

Where once we used to leaf through physical newspapers, we can directly interact with their online descendants, "pinching out" images and running video on a whim.

An interesting recurring theme through the multitude of technological advances that have affected us directly as human beings is the **enduring presence of all things visual**. As a race, humans are now producing a mind-blowing level of data every day. In fact, at the time of writing, Scandinavian research center Sintef estimates that 90 percent of all the data ever produced by the human race was generated in the last two years. Yet despite this, Web usage is still dominated by visual content. Simply perform a Web search through Google or Bing, and you'll see that they present their search results as a list of Web pages, images, and video. They understand we have become more and more keyed into the power and immediacy of the visual to ensure you keep coming back for more.

Without doubt, we are a visual species.

Pace of life

100.0 mph

A Word of Warning (1)

Despite (or perhaps because of) our growing reliance on images, we also risk cheapening them. In the not too distant past, sourcing and using an image was part of the challenge of pulling together a presentation. It could entail a frustrating few hours carefully considering the best way to visualize your message. But by the time you had hunted it down and either purchased the rights or created the visual yourself, it was with a confidence that the time invested had resulted in the very best image for the job.

Sadly, it is all too easy today to make snap decisions on images thanks to the vast array available to you via search engines like Google and Bing, as well as popular image libraries like Shutterstock and iStockphoto. With a few clicks of a mouse, you're given access to some of the largest image collections in the world with the option to search on size and resolution. It's doubtlessly quick and simple to use, but there is a very real danger inherent in the ease of this process. For one thing, presentation designers can fall into the trap of using images without really considering whether they're the best choice (is there another image that provides a stronger, more enduring message to your audience?). For another, it can prompt them to opt for a visual cliché (much more on the curse of the cliché on page 142).

As demonstrated by the power of visual subtext, images need incredibly careful consideration. Choosing the most generic or the easiest accessed may well limit the effectiveness of your presentation.

One way of enforcing sufficient thought before using an image is to attach a value to it. It is interesting to see the behavioral change in our customers when they are footing the bill for an image. Quite understandably, they ponder the value and impact of the image for a notably longer time than if it had been free of charge.

Technology has granted us access to a vast array of great quality images, many of which can be used as valuable visuals within a presentation. The trick is using the time afforded by quick, easy access to images to ensure you take time to properly ponder the options and choose the right one. It's no more complex than that.

A Word of Warning (2)

Be under no illusion—the democratization of content through search engines like Google and Bing doesn't mean that you can download and use the images you find on the Web without considering who owns the rights to them.

Each of the pictures thrown up on an "images," Flickr, or on an individual website search belong to someone. The good news is that some of these kind folks allow you to use these images for your own work, completely free of charge (or for a nominal fee). The bad news is that some strictly forbid it and will pursue you through the highest courts to protect their intellectual property. The *really* bad news is that this might be the case even if there is not an explicit warning telling you that the image is subject to copyright restrictions.

Of course, the use of pictorial images is one thing. The ante only increases when you start using companies' logos and branding. Businesses (quite rightly) protect their brands with real fervor, so tread with extreme caution every time you consider adding a logo to your presentation.

Copying and pasting images from the Web is a dangerous game to play. Not only is it a legal minefield that could carry significant financial and reputational penalties, but it also has the potential to short cut the review and consideration process. The worst case scenario is that you end up with a presentation visual that not only lands you in legal hot water but also fails to deliver your message in the most compelling or engaging way. No one wins.

For these reasons, my advice is to steer clear of the temptations of Google and Bing and treat the visual element of your presentation as an investment. Image library sites like Shutterstock, iStockphoto, and Fotolia now offer millions of images in a range of different resolutions and formats at extremely competitive costs. With these sites now competing for the everyday presenter's business, the average price per image has reduced to the point where there simply is no excuse for being cheap and (potentially) stealing images from Google and Bing.

So, consider yourself warned.

There will be a few brave/foolish souls reading this with the attitude that "with 30 million presentations delivered every day, there is no way XYZ Megacorp is going to hunt me down for the unauthorized use of their logo."

And you know what? You're probably right—*if* you plan to do with it is to present it to a small invited audience, in a locked room, and with their signatures (ideally in blood) confirming that they will not share the content with another living soul.

The only flaw in this copyright-swerving plan is that, in reality, you are likely to e-mail a version of this presentation to your audience as a follow-up . . . who then, emboldened by your brilliant message, decide to share it with a group of *their* contacts. To ensure your presentation message gets even greater exposure, you might even post a version of it onto your website or via one of the many slide-sharing sites. Or maybe one of your audience members decides to do this on your behalf.

Even internally, great presentations become viral within a business very quickly. I've lost count of the number of times slides I have developed with one part of a business have appeared in conference presentations delivered by a completely different division. If these key slides included images that defied copyright law, my business, and that of my customer, would be liable for huge damages.

The long and short of it is that no matter how hard, you have to maintain complete control over your presentation, you are exposed if you push the envelope in terms of copyright control. Caveat emptor!

Art over Effectiveness

D₆

Element   A B C **D** E F G H

Use Stock Libraries Only When Fully Prepared

Le t's face facts: We presentation writers and designers have never had it so good. The Web brings with it a multitude of amazing tools, delivering new presentation technologies such has Prezi and SlideShare to our desks at little or no cost. Sites such as Shutterstock and iStockphoto grant us access to millions and millions of low-cost, high-quality images.

The Web has given business presenters, no matter how small their budget, access to stock photo libraries that were previously limited to big creative agencies' large wallets. Although businesses were ultimately paying for these through their hefty agency retainers, there was a real sense that the standard business presenter was not part of the inner circle and as such would have to put up with the clichéd clipart and tired images supplied in their PowerPoint image library. As a result, a generation of presentations featured dated cartoons of ducks hitting a CRT computer monitor with a mallet or cheesy handshake illustrations. Gaining access to millions of professionally shot, high-resolution images couldn't come quickly enough.

Nowadays, we face a different problem: Rather than being limited to a small pool of free clichéd images to use in our presentations, we have millions of iterations of the same clichés.

For example, try typing "handshake" into iStockphoto. It will provide you with more than 20,000 image options to review, buy, and download. Some of these will be beautifully shot—real works of art in their own rights—and some of them will be up-to-date but essentially the same clichéd version of their PowerPoint image library predecessor. Importantly, the blame for the issue doesn't lie with the good people of iStockphoto or their community photographers; it lies firmly at the doorstep of the presentation designer. Although the image options we have available to us have grown exponentially, the time we invest in really developing truly engaging visual ideas and analogies has remained static at best.

With such a deep well of resources to pull upon, writers and designers owe it to their audiences and their presentation message to invest more than a passing thought into the images they use.

Please cut out for more innovative presentations!

Over the past nine years, the team at Eyeful have pulled together a list of "don't go there" visual cliché's that we do our damndest to steer our customers away from.

Top of the list is the handshake (representing partnership, agreement, or confirmation) closely followed by target images (representing a goal, focus, or a win). Others include the overuse of signs, hands (normally clasped together in some strange combination, high-fiving or simply giving us what's apparently meant to be a comforting thumbs-up). All of these are clichés, all are way too familiar, and all point to a complete lack of original thought on behalf of the presenter.

My personal pet peeve is the use of a jigsaw image to represent a problem or the fact that elements lock together to form a complete form. The inanity of it drives me to the edge of sanity (as my colleagues, the poor souls who have to put up with my jigsaw themed rants, will bear testament to).

The good news is that there are always a wide array of alternatives available to you; they just require some investment in time to consider (plus maybe the opportunity to bounce them off colleagues to sense check them if you think you're over thinking things!).

For those short on time or short on colleagues, here are some alternatives to the clichéd images that are oh-so-easy to slip into:

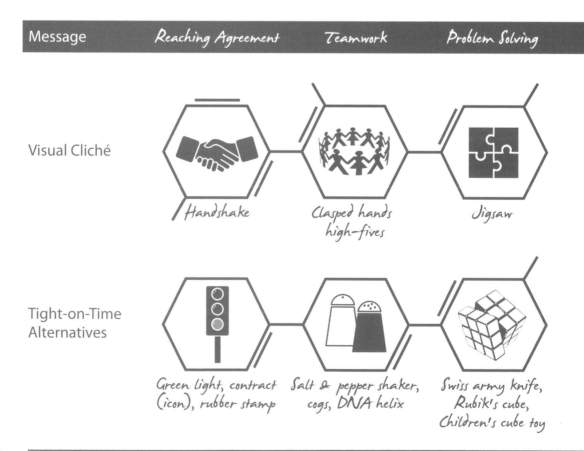

Message	Reaching Agreement	Teamwork	Problem Solving
Visual Cliché	Handshake	Clasped hands high-fives	Jigsaw
Tight-on-Time Alternatives	Green light, contract (icon), rubber stamp	Salt & pepper shaker, cogs, DNA helix	Swiss army knife, Rubik's cube, Children's cube toy

CORROSIVE CLICHÉ

Online stock libraries are extraordinarily helpful resources for today's business presenter—but they should the *final* port-of-call when pulling together your presentation. Leaping in too early can only increase your chances of jigsaw-piece-inspired-visual-clichédom.

Knowing *what* you want to say and how you want to say must be the foundations upon which you source and use imagery within your presentation. Great images do not make a great presentation if they are merely beautiful versions of tired clichés or are being used to decorate a slide rather than prompt a response or reaction from your audience.

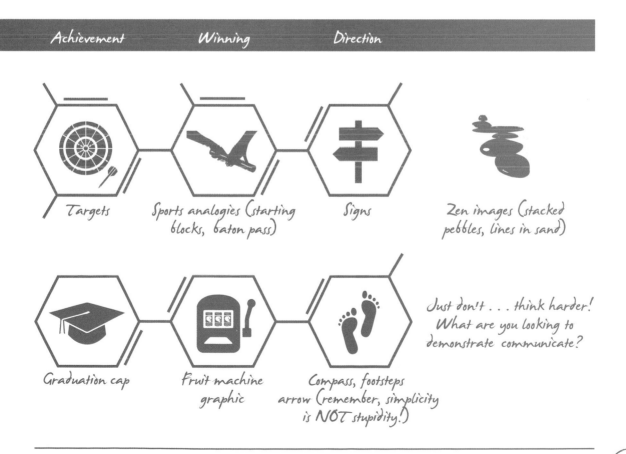

Achievement   Winning   Direction

Targets

Sports analogies (starting blocks, baton pass)

Signs

Zen images (stacked pebbles, lines in sand)

Graduation cap

Fruit machine graphic

Compass, footsteps arrow (remember, simplicity is *NOT* stupidity!)

Just don't . . . think harder! What are you looking to demonstrate communicate?

Provocative Presentations

It's very easy to make the mental leap from wanting to engage your audience with an strong, emotionally charged visual to using images that are simply there to shock. Although the use of provocative images will grab your audience's attention, there is a very high probability of sparking a "second story" from which there is no way back. It might also polarize and upset sections of your audience (reference audience profile heat map chapter) before you've had a chance to properly engage them.

There is an interesting distinction when it comes to the appropriate use of provocative visuals or props: It would seem to depend on the size and scale of your presentation. Let me explain.

Bill Gates, once of Microsoft and now famed for his philanthropy, delivered an impassioned presentation at a TED event way back in 2009. It would not be unfair to describe Bill's reputation as a public speaker as being a little downbeat. In his previous life as founder of Microsoft, he had presented himself as the epitome of the nervous techie (with generally awful PowerPoint slides to boot).

What made Bill's TED presentation so noteworthy wasn't the fact that he didn't use a bullet point–strewn PowerPoint deck or that his impassioned delivery regarding the continuing (but treatable) scourge of malaria across the planet demonstrated real oratory skills. Nope—the presentation was talked, tweeted, and rewatched online more than 1 million times primarily due to one provocative act: He released (malaria-free) mosquitos into the auditorium with the words, "there's no reason only poor people should have the experience."

It was something of a masterclass in how to fully exploit an opportunity, because it not only demonstrated great showmanship (à la Steve Jobs), but, more important, it exhibited the impact a provocative act could have on audience engagement and understanding.

Now back to reality . . .

Bill Gates can get away with this sort of thing because he's . . . well, he's Bill Gates speaking at a large TED event.

Superstar chef, TV icon, and champion for better food in schools Jamie Oliver can get away with pouring barrow loads of sugar onto the floor because he's . . . well, he's Jamie Oliver and he's speaking at a large TED event.

As a business presenter, it would at best be brave and in reality, rather foolish, to follow these examples too closely. Walking into a conventional boardroom to pitch an idea and then exposing your audience to something as provocative as a jar of mosquitos or a barrow load of sugar will simply not work. In a similar fashion, I've seen incredibly provocative *images* used at conferences (photography taken from war zones and famine struck countries) that resonated with everyone in the large auditorium but would simply be too harsh and direct for a smaller audience. The intimacy you quickly build when presenting to a small audience can become uncomfortable equally speedily.

The use of valuable visuals makes it possible to grab and then sustain your audience's attention. The trick is to turn the dial up or down depending on the audience profile and the type of presentation you are delivering.

One size does not fit all.

PRESENTATION GIMMICKS

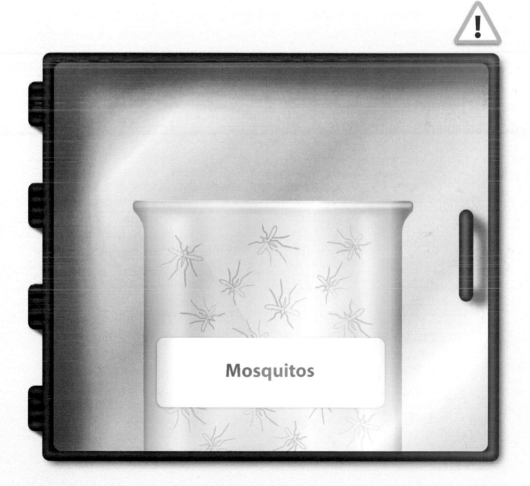

Mosquitos

A Word about Infographics

Definition: An infographic is a visualization of data or ideas that tries to convey complex information to an audience in a manner that can be quickly consumed and easily understood.

Mark Smiciklas
The Power of Infographics: Using Pictures to Communicate and Connect with Your Audiences

Over the past few years, infographics have started to pop up in the most unlikely of places. From magazines to posters to animated films on YouTube, it's not uncommon to be greeted with some form of infographic covering a dazzling array of topics.

Thankfully, I'm all in favor of infographics becoming more of our everyday life. They make navigating the London Tube network simple, make setting up new technology at home an absolute breeze, and aid my understanding of local election results (normally employed by an overexcited presenter on an elaborate TV set). The clever and often very beautiful graphic design, simple thinking, and logical content structure makes our lives easier and more attractive to the eye day in, day out.

Where I do struggle with the use of infographics, however, is in presentations. As the use of this design approach has increased in popularity and profile, they have started to find their way into presentation decks on an alarmingly frequent basis. It may be a short-lived fad among those presenters who feel they need to project a "finger on the pulse" image, but the reality is that it compromises both the presentation *and* the infographic.

The reason for this is simple: By their very nature, good infographics tell their audience pretty much **the whole story**. Because they operate independently of a presenter, they need to share way more content than is healthy for a visual slide.

This is not to say that infographics are not aesthetically pleasing; they usually are. It's just that their structure, format, and copious amounts of content leaves no opportunity for a meaningful engagement with the audience.

As with all things presentation-based, there is an exception to the rule. It's possible to employ infographics effectively when the presentation is little more than a stand-alone document. This is most likely to take on an electronic form (either as a series of self explanatory slides, a video, or hosted on the Web as a SlideShare file), but the distinguishing factor is that there is no presenter to support the sharing of information or driving home the key message.

Infographics in presentations act in exactly the same way as they do independently: They are there to clearly communicate facts in a logical way. For example, I have seen infographic techniques used very effectively when presenting publicly quoted company results. In these situations, there is no intention of building engagement with an audience or referencing different profiles—it's purely about the broadcast of simple information. Nothing more, nothing less.

With the Presentation Lab's aim of delivering a long-term sticky message to your audience, this lack of audience engagement puts the infographic approach at the back of the queue when it comes choosing valuable presentation visuals.

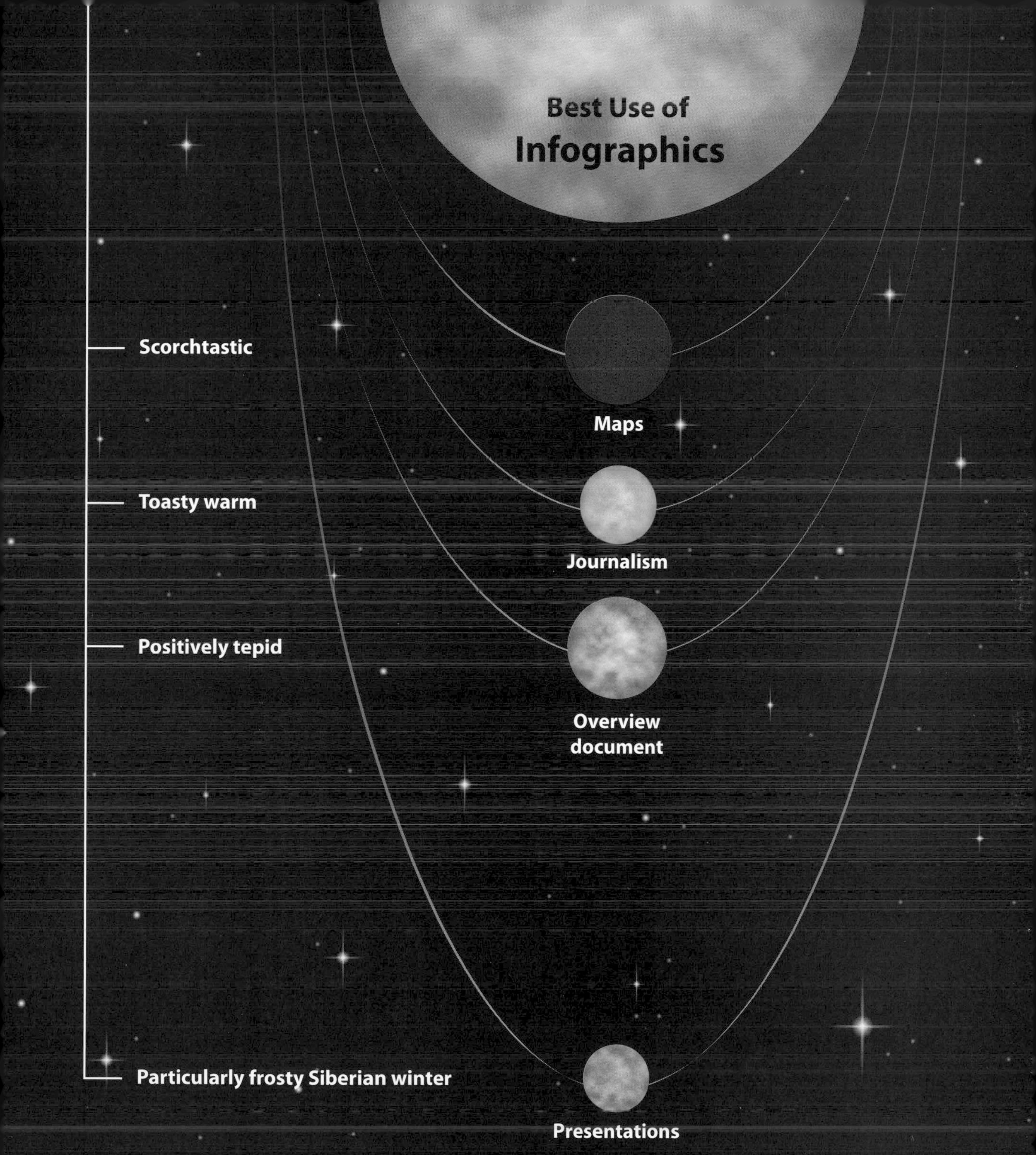

Best Use of
Infographics

Scorchtastic

Maps

Toasty warm

Journalism

Positively tepid

Overview
document

Particularly frosty Siberian winter

Presentations

Dealing with Data

D₇

Element   A B C **D** E F G H

Ba sed on the information shared thus far, it would very easy to assume that, as long as you are armed with the courage to think beyond the standard form of bullet points and clip art, creating presentation visuals is relatively straightforward. The casual reader may mistakenly assume that simply ditching the image clichés and taking time out to ponder the best use of visuals as part of a presentation will put him or her well on the way to creating presentation visuals that inspire, engage, and communicate clearly to audiences.

But the reality for many presentations is somewhat different.

Many presentations, both internal and external, are easily bogged down in a deluge of data and silos of statistics. These typically manifest themselves in hyper detailed content accompanied with busy and complex slide decks. The real tell tale sign for a presentation of this ilk is when the presenter utters the immortal words, "*You won't be able to see this at the back of the room so let me explain it to you.*" There are few things more likely to kill an audience's engagement dead in its tracks than these 20 words.

The good news is that it *doesn't need* to be like this. Data-heavy content, and ergo, the accompanying visuals, follow pretty much the same Presentation Optimization rules as other formats:

1. You need a **strong message** around which to build your story.

2. This message needs to be supported with **relevant content**.

3. This content needs to be **visualized in a way that connects** with your audience.

Delivering Data as a Story

No matter how much data you may be wading through in the preparation phase, your presentation still very much needs to deliver a structured story. And this story must move your audience to *do something* with the information you've shared—make a decision, change a viewpoint, or consider alternatives. Frankly, merely throwing unstructured data at them will do you or your message no favors.

The most important responsibility you have as a presenter is to guide your audience through the story, pointing them in the right direction for them to understand, and, ideally, embrace and act upon your message.

Today's presentation grandmasters know how to build data into their message. Rather than becoming an obstacle that they need to negotiate or seeing it as 'the boring part,' they let the data form the backbone of the story.

Consider the Following:

Gross domestic product (GDP) across African nations is growing at unprecedented levels. According to the World Bank, the countries with the highest growth levels in 2012 were as follows:

World's 10 fastest-growing economies

Although impressive, these statistics are still a little too dry for regular consumption. Presenting this information at a conference, an internal strategy meeting, or school education event might prompt a few nodding heads and the odd thoughtful stroke of a beard . . . but little else.

Percentage of annual average GDP growth 2012 %

1. Sierra Leone	**18.2**
2. Mongolia	12.3
3. Niger	**11.2**
4. Panama	10
5. Ivory Coast	**9.8**
6. Burkina Faso	**9**
7. Papua New Guinea	9
8. Ethiopia	**8.5**
9. Lao PDR	8.3
10. Uzbekistan	8.2

SOURCE: WORLD BANK

Creating Compelling Content

But by putting this information into context with your audience's frame of reference, the data suddenly takes on a whole new dimension.

It's still based on factually sound data and can still stand up to scrutiny—but you can now apply it in a way that will resonate with your audience. You have the basis of a story that can support your presentation message. What does this information mean to your audience, their livelihoods and their families? What are the opportunities? What are the threats?

All these questions (and their answers) can now start to form the story backbone of your presentation and help you deliver a message that will stick with your audience going forward.

Supporting Data Content

Just because you have the data doesn't mean you have to share it all with your audience. As highlighted in both the Message and Content sections of this book, simplicity is not stupidity. Cut out the noise, and your audience will hear your message a lot more clearly.

Charts in particular have an unnerving ability to collect clutter—unnecessary gridlines, distracting backgrounds, overlapping elements, way too much information, and so on. Give your chart the opportunity to breathe and allow your audience to engage with the information that makes the difference to the story.

However, your quest for simplicity and clarity should not come at the expense of honesty or transparency. You'll need to have the confidence to stand by your data when someone questions it. You'll also want to be able to sleep at night, so massaging the visualization of data is a dangerous game to play.

From this . . .

Our brand market share

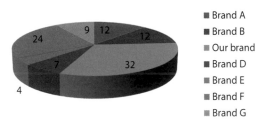

- Brand A
- Brand B
- Our brand
- Brand D
- Brand E
- Brand F
- Brand G

To this . . .

Our brand market share

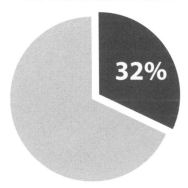

Sticking to the Facts

This is an extraordinary example of how to visually simplify data while simultaneously pulling the wool over the eyes of your audience.

Chart clarity evangelist Jon Moon is always on the lookout for suspect (and often amusing) graphical interpretations. Take the example of Scottish football team Glasgow Rangers who have had a tough time of late. This is a representation of an actual chart used to show their season ticket sales apparently zooming to new heights, despite their bad fortune. Yet look closer at the numbers and you'll easily spot a couple of key errors.

First, the absence of a y-axis allows the sign makers to visually overstate the upsurge in sales somewhat. (Did the chart demonstrate to you a mere 0.2 percent increase in sales between the 11/12 and 12/13 seasons? Nope, me neither.) Also, the chart is simply wrong. The drop in numbers between the 10/11 season and the 11/12 season is disproportionately small compared with the increased between 11/12 and 12/13.

Playing with the way you display data is not only misleading; it could also leave you in very hot water. So tread carefully.

Playing with the way you display data is not only misleading, but it could leave you in very hot water. Tread carefully.

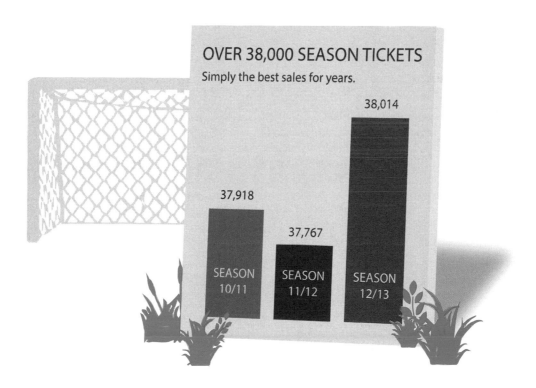

OVER 38,000 SEASON TICKETS
Simply the best sales for years.

38,014

37,918

37,767

SEASON 10/11   SEASON 11/12   SEASON 12/13

Getting Your Data Noticed

Your audience deserves the same standard of clarity around the data you present as the rest of your presentation content. A well-crafted presentation that encompasses all the elements of Presentation Optimization is destined to struggle (and perhaps even fail) if you deliver key factual/data elements in a cluttered and uncompelling manner.

To ensure data doesn't become your presentation Achilles heel, you need to visualize data in ways that your audience will quickly understand and with which they're able to engage. Conventional charts are an obvious avenue to explore, and can be very powerful visual tools when developed carefully.

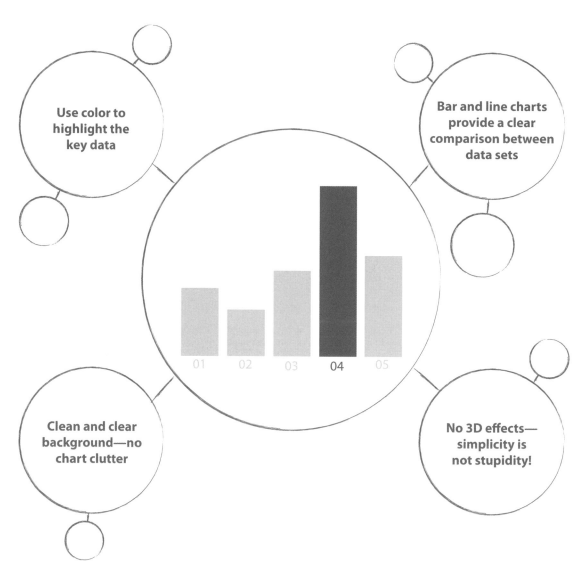

Use color to highlight the key data

Bar and line charts provide a clear comparison between data sets

Clean and clear background—no chart clutter

No 3D effects— simplicity is not stupidity!

However, in line with our mantra of constantly pushing the boundaries in the Presentation Lab, consider some other options.

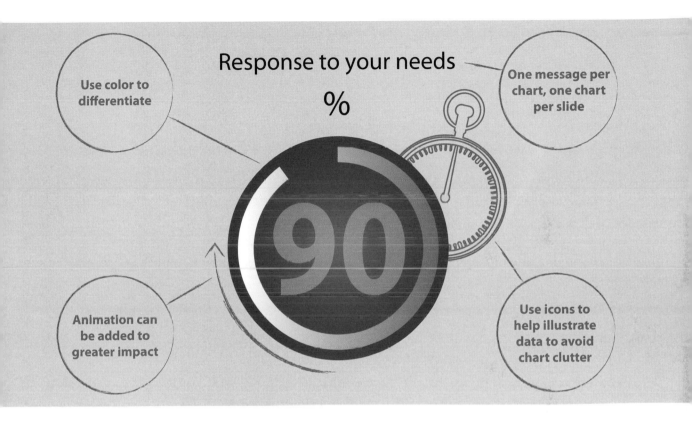

Data can be a little daunting to many presenters, myself included. It tends to come in complex, dense tables and spreadsheets and can initially make it a challenge to see the forest for the trees. By far the easiest way to get over this initial panic is to recognize one simple thing: Data is content in the same way that text on a slide is content.

As such, just as you work hard to trim back the clutter of too many words on a slide, so should you take the same approach with data and statistics.

In summary, the best way to visually enhance data-heavy slides is to follow that most important of all presentation teachings:

Keep it simple.

The buzz you get from identifying the right visual to help share your message with your identified audience is mighty satisfying. It brings with it a confidence that will put you in good stead as you prepare to deliver your presentation. All is good with the world.

Your task is to now take this visual concept and convert it into a powerful and useful presentation tool. Despite the plethora of presentation software available, chances are that your first port of call will be PowerPoint or Keynote.

Please heed this advice: Step away from the computer until you have "storyboarded" your presentation.

Storyboarding is the process of committing your story, content, and visuals to paper before making the final transition over to PowerPoint, Prezi, or whichever slideware takes your fancy. The simple act of drawing the slides out allows you to continue the all important process of building your presentation with your audience at the core of your thinking.

Manually completing the slide by hand will also prompt you to consider how much content clutter you are adding to your presentation. If you start to suffer from writer's cramp or are forced to write small to squeeze it all in, chances are that you've got too much information on the slide!

At Eyeful Presentations, we use a simple storyboard format to prompt a step away from PowerPoint and get all parties involved thinking visually. All the boring technical information regarding animations, screen ratios, and hyperlinks is set to one side, allowing the important job of visualizing the content to be the focus of our attention.

Now armed with a paper-based storyboard that will help you share your message through powerful visuals, you're ready to move the final stage of the process—delivering your presentation.

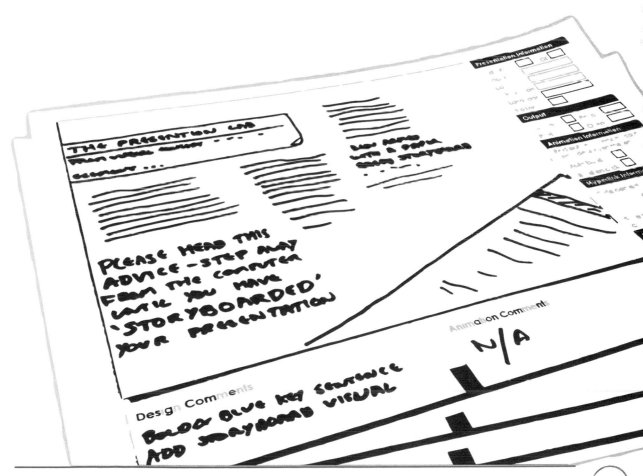

In Conclusion

D₉

Element   A B C **D** E F G **H**

Visuals have the power to move an audience.

They can stir powerful emotions, which can elevate your presentation from the ordinary to the stuff of legend. There's no getting away from it: 99.9 percent of presentations, no matter what their format, deliver greater results when supported by strong visuals that engage with your audience.

Chosen carefully, visuals support and "lock in" your message to the point where it can be easily shared with others, often without any prompting from you.

By the same token, using the wrong image—clichéd, inconsistent, or simply for shock value—can scupper your presentation before you're even out of the starting blocks.

Now is the time to embrace the power and value visuals bring to your presentation. I promise—your audiences will be forever grateful.

Message

Delivering the Final Results

E

Element   A B C D **E** F G H

PowerPoint, the Shed, & an Electric Screwdriver

E₁

Element   A B C D **E** F G H

One of the things that has baffled me for many a long year is the complete and utter obsession business presenters have with PowerPoint. When they are not slamming it for dumbing down business communication, they are holding it firmly to their chests like a comfort blanket as soon as anyone utters the word *presentation*.

It's all rather bemusing.

The following sections contain the "punch line" to everything we've been working up to during each stage of the Presentation Lab process. From the clarification of objectives to creating an audience-centric sticky message and then supporting this with content and visuals that add real value, we've been rattling toward the selection of the **presentation tool**.

I bet you thought that was going to be PowerPoint. And although you're not wrong, per se, that's just *one* of the options.

Don't get me wrong; PowerPoint is great in many situations. Despite there being a vast array of great new presentation technologies available to us, my company and its band of expert designers still do the vast majority of their valuable visual creation in PowerPoint (with a fair sprinkling of Photoshop and Illustrator thrown in to keep things looking super fresh).

It's a wonderful tool, *but* not always the most appropriate. Any seasoned salesperson is familiar with that sinking feeling the lone prospect experiences when the salesperson makes it clear that he's about to deliver his creds PowerPoint presentation. It's possible, even likely, to kill any rapport, engagement, and warmth you may have developed with the prospect as soon as you look like you're going to put a computer and a series of slides between the two of you. It's not that that they don't want you to have any visual support as you present; it's just that you've turned quite a friendly, intimate chat into a pitch.

By the same token, there are many larger prospect audiences that would look at you askance if you considered pitching to them *without* using PowerPoint (or Keynote, if that is your want).

It's about using the right tool at the right time. And this brings to mind a personal story.

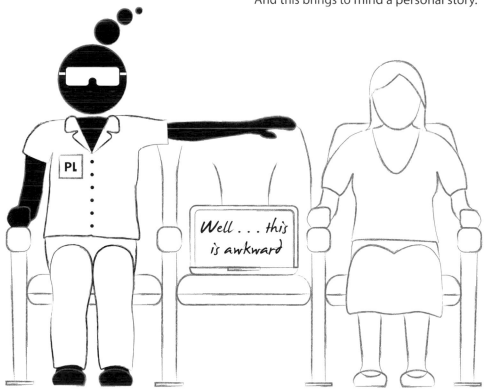

As I have galloped toward middle age, becoming a father and managing director, I've found solace (and quiet) in the simple joys of gardening. It seems not long ago that the very idea of pottering around a garden would fill me with dread, but now I'm a man obsessed with soil types, hard landscaping, and sheds.

I had always assumed that the garden shed was a typically British thing. The idea of a man and his shed is well known and regarded in the United Kingdom, with males of a certain age seeing them as a bolt hole, a place of solace, their own private space. Some men go as far as adding heating, a small fridge (typically filled with beer), and some comfy but suitably unfashionable furniture. After checking with friends in other countries, it would seem that these outside man caves are commonplace across the world—and indeed, something to be proud of.

So came the time when I decided that I needed a shed and dutifully scoured the Internet for a suitable building. Three days after ordering, the shed arrived and my heart beat just a little bit faster (mainly because it was the most flat-packed thing I have ever seen. It might have been easier to simply chop down a tree).

Undeterred, my wife and I set aside most of the following weekend to construct the shed. We warned our children to keep a safe distance to avoid being hit with either flying pieces of wood or bad language. And so we began.

Because I can never turn down a bargain or refuse purchasing a new man toy, I was able to bring many tools to this shed-building party. Never has such a small project had so many tools made available to it—from an array of clamps, drills, and spirit levels, to hammers, set squares, and chisels, to the most prized possession of these: my faithful old electric screwdriver.

Aaaaah—my electric screwdriver. It's been with me for many years, from the first time my wife and I attempted (and failed) to put up shelves in our first apartment together, to successfully mounting pictures of our two children. It's a dependable friend that's never far from my side.

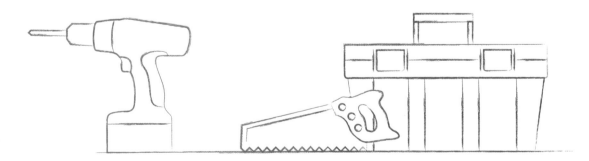

Delivering the Final Results

And this is part of the problem. Despite having a vast array of different tools, all specifically designed for the separate stages of shed building, I ended up repeatedly using the electric screwdriver. Not only does it drive screws in (as you'd expect), it's also heavy enough to knock shed side panels together, tap nails in, and take the top off paint tins.

In short, I ignored all the tools I had at my disposal and went back to the one tool I had always used—*despite* knowing that it was the wrong tool for the job, and that I had other choices that might have worked better (had I only given them a chance).

The purpose of this somewhat tortured and tenuous story is that business presenters the world over are doing exactly the same thing. They keep returning to PowerPoint as their presentation tool of choice despite there being far better options for them—and more important, for their audience.

It was this realization that prompted our final experiment—Blended Presenting.

What Is Blended Presenting?

E₂

As you know by now, the entire presentation optimization process is built on one simple goal: attaining the highest degree of **audience engagement**.

Yet, despite all this focus on audience-centric messaging, years of conditioning within business have led the vast majority of you to immediately turn to PowerPoint, or at a push, Apple's equivalent, Keynote, as the tool of choice.

The Blended Presenting stage of the process implores you to consider the wide array of Visual Engagement Tools. This does not mean dropping that "old faithful" PowerPoint completely and swapping it for the new kid on the block. It means having a presentation story that's strong enough that you're able to use *whatever* tool best suits your audience to get the message across.

For sales professionals, it is about realizing that your best collateral is your intimate and confident knowledge of the material, **not** the fancy looking PowerPoint deck you have on your laptop.

For marketers, it means deriving your power and confidence in front of an audience from your ability to visually share your story and demonstrate your points in a multitude of different ways. It means realizing that this power does *not* come from the fact that your department spent a lot of money creating an iPad app that does little more than your old company PowerPoint did.

For internal presentations, it's about truly opening up and emotionally engaging with your colleagues through visually supported stories—*not* hiding behind the prepackaged content the head office sent down to which you have little or no emotional attachment.

PRESUNTÅSHUN BLËNDIJNG

IDEA

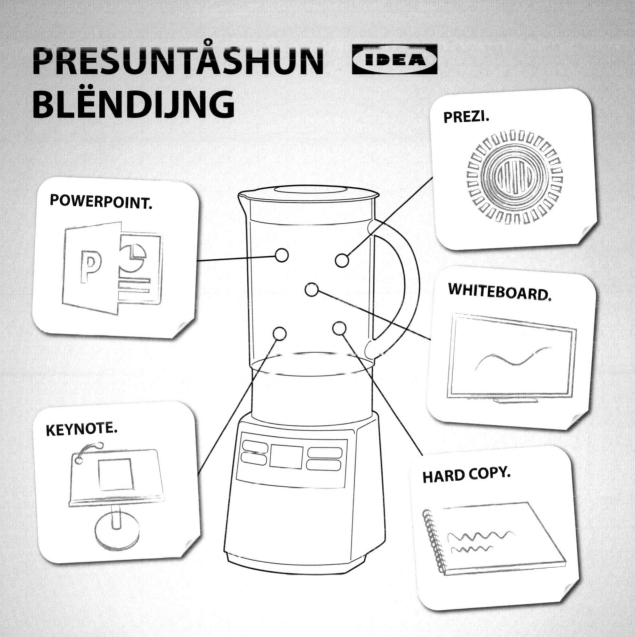

POWERPOINT.

PREZI.

WHITEBOARD.

KEYNOTE.

HARD COPY.

Most important, it's about audiences getting the respect they deserve from a presenter who feels compelled to deliver their message in the most visually engaging way they can to suit your needs.

In short, Blended Presenting is about **letting the audience and your story take center stage**—and *then* using the visual engagement tools you have available to you appropriately.

THE PRESENTATION LAB

Understanding the Presentation Landscape

Element   A B C D **E** F G H

E₃

We scratched the surface of one of the biggest omissions of the presentation sector way back in the introduction of the Presentation Lab, namely, that the vast majority of advice focuses on **formal presentations** rather than recognizing the other potential forms that business presentations take. Now, with Blended Presenting firmly in mind, it's time to revisit the Presentation Landscape.

There's no getting away from it; bookstores, social media, and the Web are awash with great advice to support the business presenter. Type "help with business presentations" into Google, and you're greeted with more than 100 million results.

The good news is that most of these links will offer considered, practical advice to help you navigate your way through a formal presentation. They'll no doubt provide hints and tips on how to stand, project your voice, and ensure that your PowerPoint slides look good. If you're wearing a suit, presenting to an audience that knows not to ask any questions until the end of the presentation, and are determined only to use PowerPoint as a visual aid, you're in good hands.

The bad news is that most business presentations are nothing like this.

Indeed, most of the day-to-day presentation situations in which you'll find yourself in do not lend themselves to the (many) rules that surround formal presentations. You'll often be presenting to a single individual over an informal coffee or to a group on a topic that needs greater levels of interaction than a linear PowerPoint slide deck will support. You might be next up on stage at a conference, and can tell from the coma-like expressions of the conference audience that another 30 slide PowerPoint deck would push them over the edge.

Whatever the particular details, more and more presentation situations exist outside of this "formal" environment.

Yet pretty much the entire canon of presentation thinking remains transfixed on addressing the shortcomings of the "I speak; you listen" format.

How Does the Presentation Landscape Break Down?

As with all good things in the presentation world, the landscape breaks down rather nicely into three key areas shown in the graphic below:

Formal	Interactive	Informal
Conferences Board meetings Bids or pitches	Online seminars Demonstrations Sales scenarios Exhibitions	Face-to-face chats

And although they aren't hard-and-fast rules, there are some basic parameters we can use to determine which kinds of presentations might fit into each area.

The Formal Presentation

As already highlighted, the Formal presentation is the traditional setting for PowerPoint, Keynote, and the multitude of other presentation software packages. Used properly, these tools can be incredibly powerful and guide an equally formal audience down your chosen path, to a mutually satisfying conclusion.

Typical presentation scenarios that fall into the Formal category are bids and pitches, conferences, and investor presentations. They have one thing in common: The presenter speaks and the audience listens, and then (ideally) a lively Q&A session kicks off at the conclusion of the presentation at the behest of the presenter. In short, the majority of the presentation is a **broadcast** rather than a **conversation**.

If it seems that I'm a little snooty about Formal presentations or that I feel they lack an intimacy that plays well with audiences, please know that this couldn't be further from the truth. Getting Formal presentations right is *hard*—damned hard. This is because these kinds of presentations, more than any other, are subject to disengaged audiences. They also frequently have more at stake, which inadvertently but understandably puts the presenter at a disadvantage before they've even stepped onto the stage. Formal presentations are also more likely to be one-offs or delivered irregularly, which means that studious rehearsal is required by all involved (and, lest we forget, most of the intended rehearsal time will be eaten up by last minute changes to the slides—an unavoidable part of human nature).

My semi-snooty tone might come from the fact that the formal presentation structure has been foisted on presenters and audiences alike for way too long. We've followed the unwritten (and in some cases, *written*) rules regarding posture, diction, and how many bullet points you're allowed on a slide so slavishly that they've hindered audience engagement.

Communication—the primary goal of most presentations—is, ironically, the first casualty of overformalization.

So how do we fix this? Being a little more casual with *all* presentations is foolish, because some do demand the formal approach. However, a good place to start is to recognize that not all presentations fit the same mold.

This leads rather nicely onto our next category: the Interactive presentation.

The Interactive Presentation

The ability to interact has never been so widely embraced as it is today. Our media thrives on its ability to engage and interact with its audiences, from the occasionally hysterical discussion boards on newspaper websites, to the hoards of business Tweeters and Facebookers, to the ease of voting contestants on and off reality TV shows (my children don't believe a Saturday evening in front of the TV is complete if they haven't called a premium rate phone line to vote off a dancer/singer/juggler who doesn't meet their high standards).

With interaction being so prevalent across the media landscape, it seems strange that presentations have, on the whole, managed to dodge the trend. It might be that conventional wisdom scorns the idea of an audience asking questions throughout a presentation; heaven forbid they got ideas above their station and started driving the presentation toward something that actually *appealed* to them. Or it might be that presenters have preferred to stay within the lines and stick with the formal approach.

Interestingly, of all the new forms of interaction, Twitter has been the one to build at least a *semblance* of a relationship with presentations. Sharing Twitter hashtags as a way of sharing thoughts and information is now standard practice at conferences and seminars. Although it's something we must approach with care—as the following story demonstrates.

There is an apocryphal tale of this concept of including Twitter-based interaction going horribly wrong at a conference—a tale that sends shivers down the spine of any business presenter. The conference organizers thought that it would be good to have a feed of all the conference-hashtagged tweets projected onto a screen as each speaker presented.

In theory, it's a fine idea, because it allows people to offer their own thoughts and insights as the presenters delivered their findings. And so it was—until one of the speakers, well, bored the audience with a confused message—one with way too much content and incredibly text-heavy slides.

"I'm bored already and it's just the first slide" came the first broadcast tweet, projected proudly onto the screen behind the presenter.

"What the hell does this mean?!" came another.

"This guy sucks," came the next.

And so it continued throughout the poor speaker's presentation. If anything, it gathered pace and turned into nothing short of a car crash until the conference organizer turned off the live feed.

Another reason for the lack of interactivity in presentations is that presenters are simply not aware that many presentation tools at their disposal are eminently capable of supporting an interactive audience engagement.

The starting off point is ultimately less about the tools you choose to use and more about the decision to move away from the Formal approach's comfort zone. When we embrace the Interactive approach we must rethink the rules and allow a presentation to become more about *discussion* than broadcast. This apparent lack of control demands that the presenter has a much greater grasp of the presentation story and message, an intimate knowledge of the tool, and an awareness of the audience and how and when to react to their engagement.

This reminds me of a project we carried out for Microsoft in the United Kingdom many years ago. We had been asked to support a team developing an internal presentation that shared the results of a long-term efficiency study.

As you might imagine, Microsoft is stuffed to the rafters with very intelligent and inquisitive people. There was no doubt that the audience to whom our contacts would be presenting were going to want to question, delve into, and interrogate the findings. As such, taking the standard formal approach to the presentation project seemed a little too rigid to ensure proper audience engagement. After discussing the matter with the project team, we threw out the concept of a linear presentation and replaced it with a fully interactive PowerPoint presentation using custom shows and an intuitive menu system.

We went to work to develop the structure that would support this approach. We ended up creating a powerful interactive toolkit presentation using nothing more than PowerPoint. No fancy widgets, no code scripting, and no expensive plug-ins, just PowerPoint.

Perhaps most memorable was the shocked cries of "How the hell did you get PowerPoint to do that?! That's amazing!" from our customer—the same customer who had been part of the team that *owned, developed, and sold PowerPoint* to millions of business presenters all over the world.

If this doesn't highlight how much of our chosen slideware's capabilities we waste, I don't know what does!

Make no bones about it: As the presenter, you are still in charge of the process and need to navigate the presentation and your audience from A to B. The only difference with the Interactive model is that you may meander off-course occasionally if and when a given topic proves of particular interest to your audience. But as long as you complete the journey and end up at point B with message duly delivered and understood, then it really doesn't matter how circuitous a route your audience may have taken you. You've still succeeded.

The good news is that it's not as scary as it sounds! A good interactive presentation requires as much from the presenter as a business conversation. You simply need to know your subject—because there's no opportunity to simply read words from the slide autocue style—and be ready to listen to your audience.

As such, the best opportunities to move from a Formal to Interactive presentation style are exhibitions, demonstrations, and account management sales meetings. It's less about delivering a slick pitch and more about building a bond and rapport and demonstrating you can support your audience.

It's for these reasons that interactive presentations tend to work best for smaller audience groups. Any more than five audience members and you can find yourself in the middle of an argument rather than a conversation. At this point, you'll be better served by calling upon the more traditional rules of the Formal approach.

The question remains—why eschew the well-established Formal approach for the apparently more risky Interactive route? The answer is simple: **audience engagement**.

Ultimately the reason we present is to *engage with the audience* to the point where they will listen to, understand, and ideally act on our message. By putting them in the driver's seat and allowing them into the presentation conversation, you dramatically change the dynamics of the presenter-audience relationship. You're giving them license to test, question, and evaluate your message as part of the process. By doing so, you're much more likely to keep the audience on your side and thus to get the result you desire.

The Informal Presentation

Paradoxically, this is both the most natural form of communication but also the most difficult presentation approach to get right. The Informal presentation still requires sufficient structure to guide the presenter and their audience from A to B. However, you must do so in a way that does not impact the cozy/nonthreatening environment that both parties enjoy.

The example I always use is the ubiquitous airport bar conversation. You're unwinding with a beer while waiting for your flight to board when you strike up a conversation with the person next to you. As businesspeople do, you ask each other what line of work you're in and the reason for your travel. One thing leads to another, and soon enough you're sharing your business message with your new friend—just like you had done three hours prior to a room of prospects.

The power of the Informal presentation is that rather than pulling out your laptop and firing up PowerPoint—thereby killing the nice, informal environment you've created—you're able to tell/sell your story using no more than a napkin and a pen by way of visuals.

Note: The use of handmade impromptu visuals as part of an Informal engagement is not restricted to bars! It's a running joke in our offices that I find it difficult to chat with anyone without a pad of paper and selection of pens at hand. I'm always doodling to visually share my thoughts and ideas with someone. Despite the jokes, people understand that this is my informal way of presenting and engaging with the team, and ultimately ensuring that they understand and receive my message loud and clear.

It's essential to know that using an Informal approach works only if the presenter really knows their subject. This is more than aimless doodling and a meandering story; it's about recognizing that the engagement with the audience demands a more relaxed approach, while still delivering a focused and powerful message.

Lest We Forget . . . Remote Presentations

In addition to these face-to-face presentation approaches, we must also give a nod to the ever-increasing remote forms of presenting—be that as a one-to-one Web presentation, larger webinar groups, or recorded presentations on platforms such as SlideShare and YouTube.

There's no doubt that attempting to cover all these options in a chapter of a book not only would be silly but would be selling you short. It's a huge topic that demands a book all of its own. However, there are some basic rules to bear in mind should you find yourself delivering to a webcam in an empty office:

1. When in doubt, follow the Formal presentation format's rules.

If you think interaction is difficult enough to pull off when you're face to face with your audience, it's nearly impossible when talking to a virtual audience—no matter how many Chat and Hands Up buttons your software provider may have bestowed upon you.

2. You're fighting temptation from a variety of distractions every minute you're speaking.

When presenting face to face, you'll have a strong sense of when the audience is engaged—and when they are not. Most audiences are well mannered and courteous enough to rarely allow you to see them checking their e-mail, logging onto Facebook, or tucking into their lunch. However, all these social graces leave the room when you're not in their presence—and you and your presentation are fighting for their attention.

The solution is simple: Make your presentation more interesting than their Facebook buddies!

3. Murphy's Law—no matter how well you prepare, incidents will happen.

Every seasoned remote presenter has a war story about the time the broadband connection failed them or their prospect's firewall blocked them out of the network. They're like badges of honor (of which I have several).

From a technical standpoint, about all you can do is check the connection, rehearse with your contact wherever possible, and keep your fingers crossed. There are, however, some situations against which you *can* guard yourself. I recall attending a remote presentation from a vendor who was working from home. Everything was going to plan until we suddenly heard a door open very loudly and a child's voice proclaim, "Mom, I need to use the bathroom really badly." (Such are the joys of remote presenting and parenting.) If nothing else, locking your door and letting your family know what you're doing is a good first step!

Note: If the presentation is so important that you simply cannot allow it to fail, jump on a plane and present in person. Your audience is likely to appreciate the dedication you've shown, and you can rest easy knowing that you won't have to fight technology or marauding kids on top of the pre-presentation nerves!

Delivering Competitive Advantage

The evolving Presentation Landscape is an incredibly exciting change in the way we deliver our messages to audiences. In my opinion, it trumps any new technological developments (while the birth of the iPad/tablet was exciting, it's just another tool at the end of the day) or new design thinking.

The Presentation Landscape takes our ability to truly build a relationship with audiences to a whole new level . . . something that **no single presentation tool** will ever be able to do.

The reason for this bold statement is a simple one—it relies on people recognizing and acting on the opportunity. Once we understand the dynamics in play at any presentation situation—and use this insight to apply the right storytelling approach and tools to meet the audience's requirements—we automatically move up the scale in terms of engagement. This increased engagement provides us not only with a greater chance of meeting our objectives (remember Must-Intend-Like!), but also addressing our audience's specific needs.

There's no getting away from it: A greater understanding of the Presentation Landscape coupled with a Blended Presenting approach delivers huge competitive advantage that while useful for internal or conference presentations is *invaluable* for sales or investor presentations.

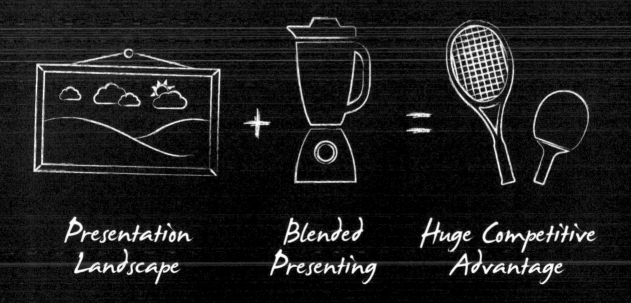

Presentation Landscape + Blended Presenting = Huge Competitive Advantage

THE PRESENTATION LAB

Blended Presenting: A Customer's Tale

E4

As news of our Presentation Optimization methodology spread, we started getting calls from international companies looking for support and guidance. These were always exciting projects that combined travel to some remarkable countries with the opportunity to work with some truly fantastic companies and people.

Of all these early international projects, there is one that stands out for a couple of reasons. We'd been working with the European offices of a German software company for a number of years, having supported them in all manner of different presentation scenarios. We'd been there for sales decks, kick off events, and for internal presentations—and we'd used PowerPoint as the visual tool each and every time.

There's no doubt that they'd categorized us as their "PowerPoint people." This suited us down to the ground; they required a lot of PowerPoint, we had a great reputation within the business and, top down, they were nice people to work with. Then the message spread to the United States.

I was asked to join a confidential conference call, where it was announced that the software company was in the process of acquiring one of their largest competitors. This acquisition would make a huge difference to the already very impressive business—a revised and improved customer proposition, greater leverage in a vibrant marketplace, and the opportunity to embed themselves even deeper into their growing customer base. It was all very exciting, and they needed a PowerPoint presentation to release as part of the rollout training and coaching for their global sales team. I was summoned to the United States and arrived at their offices fresh as a daisy after sitting in business class on my flight and being put up in one of the finest hotels the East Coast could offer.

With a suitably senior (and, let's be honest, expensive) executive team seated behind closed doors, we commenced the Presentation Optimization process. We established a good understanding of the prospect audience, discussed objectives, and quickly identified a compelling key message (it was such a wonderful proposition that none of this was all that tricky). Then we moved onto the content.

And this is where the cold sweats started.

The audience heat map profile was heavily weighted toward the Factual with a strong sense of Visionary. This was to be expected—it was a highly technical sale with a multimillion dollar price tag attached. Given the very technical nature of the new combined solution, we were going to have to get pretty detailed quite quickly in terms of content, which could alienate the visionary section of the audience. My business prides itself in getting PowerPoint to do things it wasn't originally designed to do, but this seemed like a step too far.

I had no option but to voice my concerns. So, with more than a little trepidation, I turned to my senior and generous hosts and uttered the fatal words:

"This isn't right for PowerPoint. I don't see how we can make this work using simple slides."

Somewhat understandably, a silence fell over the room. (Oh dear.)

I pressed on, however, explaining that the story itself was extremely compelling and that by sticking purely to PowerPoint, we ran the very real risk of switching off what should and would be an audience hooked on everything we had to say.

I suggested that we continue to think visually and see where the rest of the session took us. I think it's fair to say that there was a sense in the room that this had all turned a bit sour, and I was to blame. (Oh dear indeed.)

About an hour in, I had a flash of inspiration after scribbling up comments and ideas on the very fancy electronic whiteboard. I was using it to share my ideas and demonstrate visually my message, so why couldn't my customer and their sales team do the same thing?

Over the following 3 hours, we created a proposition story that could be visualized using the whiteboard. We "topped and tailed" this innovative approach using conventional PowerPoint; this not only suited the audience but also gave the presenters a familiar and defined way of starting and concluding the formal presentation.

The customer was delighted and went on to make a huge success of their new combined solution, cutting a swathe through the competition and opening up new opportunities left, right, and center.

Importantly, there were a couple of completely unforeseen benefits to this new way of presenting. It seemed that the audience was compelled to interact as the salesperson used the interactive whiteboard to tell the visual story and explain how the elements might work for their prospect; they often jumped to their feet, grabbed a marker and drew their requirements right on the board. Despite our best efforts, PowerPoint or Keynote never got close to this level of interactivity.

Add to that the fact that our customer's sales team now had a visual describing their prospects' specific requirements **in the prospect's handwriting**. This meant that they could use the wonders of Smartboards to e-mail and insert them directly into proposal documents—and could reference them later on to produce a truly bespoke offering.

From moments of blind panic came a solution that exceeded all of our expectations.

Personally, this was a sea change in the way I looked at the entire process of presenting. By challenging the established norms and mixing things up a bit, we'd made a great story even more powerful and palatable for the audience. It was a simple as using the right tool at the right time for the right type of content—and by doing so, we'd inadvertently created a new approach to presentations. Blended Presenting had been born.

We no longer view presentations as necessarily being purely of one format. Our customer base now generally accepts that getting the message and story optimized is the first and often most challenging phase in the development of a presentation. The visualization of that story into an array of different presentation outputs is the fun bit. It's what allows us to engage with any audience type, in any number, and in any situation in a way that truly makes a difference.

Suddenly, the **audience** is in charge of the format the presentation takes—and the presenter is able to call upon any number of combinations from their toolkit of formats.

It's exciting, it's relevant, and it's powerful.

Tools for the Job

E_5

So Many Ways to Engage . . .

With a firm understanding of the Presentation Landscape in hand, you can now turn your attention to the plethora of presentation tools available to you. Used properly as part of a blended approach, these tools will support your new thinking and aid that all-important engagement with your audience.

It's time to look at the tools for the job; however with so many available to the business presenter today, it can all become a little overwhelming.

Beware the New Toy . . .

Presenters the world over are subject to the constant temptation to try something new—either for the novelty factor or because it will look cutting edge to their audience.

When Apple launched the iPad, people scrambled to convert a wave of presentations from PowerPoint to Keynote (a relatively slow process in the early days of the iPad) so that executives could use their new toy at the next board meeting. While sleek and slick, the early iPads were awful if presenting to more than three people due to the lack of a VGA port. Yet people still persisted.

Online presentation tool Prezi rode on the back of being different when presenters started picking it up in early 2011. Again, the allure of zooms, whooshes, and a general step away from the norm appealed to many, despite the occasional moans from nauseous audience members.

I distinctly remember a conversation with a creative agency that had come to us for support. The lead presenter was fully aware that Prezi was the wrong tool for his audience and message, but felt compelled to employ it since "we're expected to use the latest technology."

Even though it was the wrong tool for the job? At best, it's foolhardy, at worst, it shows a complete disrespect for the audience.

What Fits Where . . . ?

Alas, there is no truly definitive list of which tool to use for different presentation scenarios. Indeed, the purpose of *the Presentation Lab* is to arm you with sufficient information to allow you to make the right choice at the right time. The beauty of having a good understanding of the Presentation Landscape, coupled with the Blended Presenting approach is that it lets you apply these tools at the most appropriate time to deliver true audience engagement.

After all, there is no reason that an informal presentation may not ultimately lead to you firing up the computer and running a PowerPoint show—**if that's what engages the audiences best**. By the same token, if it doesn't achieve that measure, you must move on to another tool.

The Blended Presenting wheel (below) is designed to offer no more than **a best practice guide**—one we've developed after working with hundreds of companies on thousands of presentations that fall into one of these three main categories.

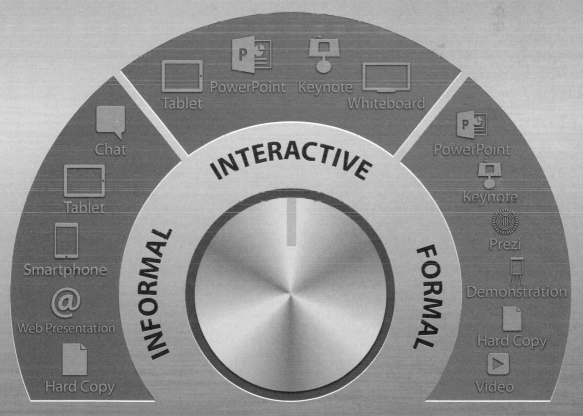

With this in mind, and to get things off to a good start, we've pulled together a list of the usual suspects in terms of presentation tools. The following section includes our diagnosis of their relative strengths, weaknesses, where and what you can use them with—and most important the audience type that matches each one best.

PowerPoint

As already discussed, PowerPoint is the weapon of choice for the vast majority of business presenters across the world. The often-quoted number is that 30 million PowerPoint presentations are created every day (and remember that this was a number at best guesstimated back in 2001!). As recently as 2012, Microsoft announced that PowerPoint was now installed on 1 billion computers globally. Inevitably, its success means that its name has become synonymous with presentations (especially bad ones!).

PowerPoint started life as a Mac tool called Forethought back in 1987, but after being bought by Microsoft (initially against Bill Gates' wishes), it gained popularity and profile on every businessperson's desktop computer.

For every fan of PowerPoint, there are 10 who deride it as a tool of mass miscommunication and the source of many of the evils of business today, namely dumbed down data and a general lack of understanding. However, this somewhat misses the point; it is simply a *piece of software*. Blaming PowerPoint for awful business presentations and communication is like blaming your TV set for the fact that there is nothing interesting to watch this evening.

The truth is somewhere in the middle; PowerPoint is neither evil nor particularly angelic. As with all of the technologies available nowadays, the sins and blessings primarily sit with the user.

What's good

PowerPoint does a lot of things very well. It's incredibly simple to use, despite more recent versions offering real power in terms of graphic manipulation and video editing.

In comparison to other tools, it's very flexible, and offers a wide range of outputs from the development of slides—video, hard copy, PDF and, with the right plug-ins, Web-friendly formats such as Flash and HTML5—that are incredibly easy to use.

In the right hands, it can also be a powerful interactive presentation tool that lets presenters "drill down" into information in line with the audiences' questions and areas of interest. As is the case with much of PowerPoint's features, most are either left undiscovered or horribly misused by would-be presentation designers.

What's not good

Paradoxically, its ease of use is what causes PowerPoint most of its issues. It's intuitive nature and wide availability compels every businessperson with Office installed on their computer to mistakenly believe that they are equipped to develop a visual presentation. For reasons already covered, crafting an engaging and impactful presentation requires so much more than pulling together some highly animated slides—and sadly, PowerPoint fools its users into a false sense of security and confidence in being able to provide this.

One of the reasons that PowerPoint gets such a hard time from disgruntled audiences is the fact that unprepared presenters fall into the trap of "vomiting" their content onto the slide with little thought for message, story or structure. Although it's slightly unfair to blame the Microsoft programmers entirely, they *could* do a bit more to support their customers (and their audiences!) by providing some hints, tips, and nudges toward presentation best practice. Instead, all they provide is a dazzling and disorientating array of background template options, and a blank bullet point slide to fill in. **People don't think in bullets; they think in pictures**. Yet PowerPoint encourages them to take this route.

Many articles, books, podcasts, and videos decry PowerPoint's shortcomings. As explained earlier, it is **not** the source of all evil.

However, it's transformation from visual presentation tool to extension of Word is an issue that all businesspeople should be aware of. More important, Microsoft's developers and programmers need to be aware of it too.

What it mixes well with

One of the best things going for PowerPoint is the level of flexibility it allows the presenter. Want to add video? No problem. Link to external sources? Ditto. Output your slides to PDF or as handouts? No sweat.

PowerPoint's flexibility often makes it the common presentation tool thread running through a Blended Presenting approach. Embedding a video into a PowerPoint slide at the appropriate point within your presentation ensures a seamless link between the two; so why wouldn't you keep it running in the background? This "Launchpad" approach seems to be the best way to think of PowerPoint. It plays nice with pretty much anything you can throw at it—even the iPad (most of the time).

When to use it

Again, PowerPoint's flexibility makes this a tricky one to answer, as it *can* be used in most situations.

We would suggest that the typical PowerPoint mentality—which sadly normally means "I talk; you listen"—is best kept to the reserve of the Formal presentation with a Q&A session at the end. This Formal environment—be it a seminar, conference, or tightly controlled sales pitch environment—is the traditional home of PowerPoint. It's what it was designed for back in 1987, and features such as speaker notes, although incredibly valuable, speak volumes (no pun intended) about the environment Microsoft still believes it belongs in today. The telltale sign is the linear deck of slides that follow each other. Although the format is perfect for the "I talk; you listen" presenter, it has the potential to quickly become a nightmare as soon as one of the audience members (often the CEO) raises a hand and asks a question "off script."

At this point, the presenter looks to the skies and asks for one of three things:

- That the ground opens and swallows him or her up

- That the number of the slide that has the answer to the question posed would spring to mind

- That PowerPoint could be an interactive tool

Thankfully, these formal presentations are becoming less and less the norm and, certainly in sales and marketing circles, a more interactive approach is gaining in popularity. This interactive scenario is where communication, storytelling, and messaging really go up a few notches, as it allows the presenter and the audience to engage to the point where a presentation becomes a conversation. PowerPoint can provide all the bells and whistles required for these situations while simultaneously applying the salve of familiarity to the nervous presenter.

We'd recommend against using PowerPoint in Informal presentations.

There's nothing that can kill the sense of bonhomie and presenter-audience rapport quicker than someone firing up a computer to deliver slide after slide of content. The one caveat here is to think about the choice of delivery tool. A well-crafted and relevant visual slide delivered via a smartphone or tablet can work well in an informal setting. Just be sure to use sparingly and with the audience and setting firmly in mind.

Who to use it with

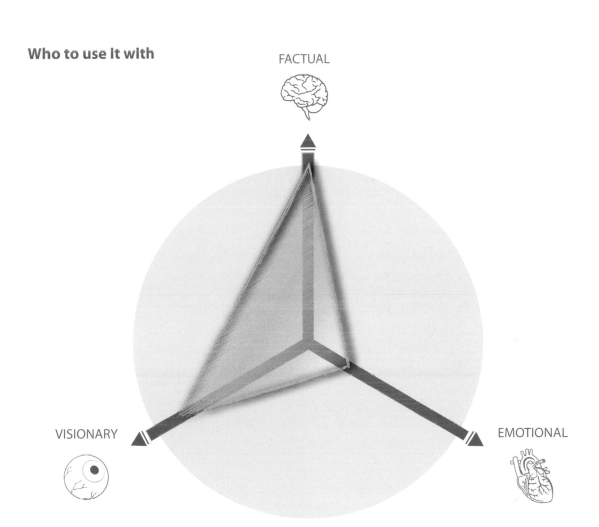

FACTUAL

VISIONARY

EMOTIONAL

How to use it

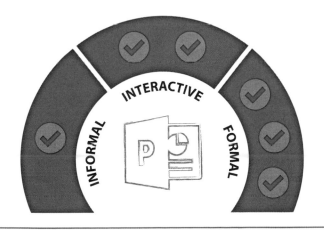

INTERACTIVE

INFORMAL

FORMAL

Keynote

Despite the intense feelings that the PowerPoint versus Keynote debate generates among the business presentation community (I'm not kidding—I've seen discussion threads disintegrate into petty name-calling as each side extols the virtues of their chosen slideware), Keynote can pretty much be summarized as Apple's take on PowerPoint.

Until the arrival of the iPad, Keynote was most closely associated with Steve Jobs and his Macworld conference presentations. The clean graphics, smooth transitions, and unique animations stood out from the crowd and certainly made PowerPoint look like the "corporate" option rather than the beautiful and engaging slides that accompanied each of Mr. Jobs' appearances.

Perhaps the biggest coup in the widespread acceptance of Keynote came with the launch of the iPad, which brought Apple's sexy new technology into the hands of business people worldwide. These very same business people wanted to use their shiny new iPads to share presentations. When they went in search of the nearest thing they could find to PowerPoint, the Keynote app won out. It's fair to say that most business people would have stayed completely oblivious to Keynote had it not been for the iPad.

Many creative agencies duly followed suit (as is the wont of any Apple disciple) and turned to Keynote as their presentation tool of choice when preparing pitches or developing presentations for their clients. And this was where some of the early issues started to rear their ugly heads.

The problem was that although the creative agencies were enjoying Keynote's visual features, their clients were firmly ensconced in a world of Microsoft office packages, including PowerPoint. Despite claims to the contrary, there was a distinct lack of compatibility between the two software packages, which became the cause of more than a few gray hairs in the creative sector. Creative agencies didn't understand or want to learn PowerPoint (there is a certain snob value at play here, too), and their customers were sticking firmly to their reliance on PowerPoint.

Since we're fortunate enough to be fluent in both Apple and Microsoft, my company continues to enjoy a steady flow of work from creative agencies still keen to distance themselves from PowerPoint, despite their customers working with it. If nothing else, it underlines the continued divide between the two most successful and popular forms of slideware. Frustrating but true.

What's good?

Sadly, it's not a completely happy ending to the story. There remain frustrating compatibility issues between the Keynote app and business's native PowerPoint files—issues with fonts, custom shows (see earlier section on Interactive presentations), and certain animations means that trepidation remains whenever one opens a Keynote presentation that originated in PowerPoint (or vice versa).

Despite countless Apple fans' protests (and I say this writing on a MacBook), Keynote and PowerPoint are practically indistinguishable. This may send shivers down the spines of both Apple and Microsoft fanboys, but it's pretty much a draw for the basic user of either presentation tool.

One of the areas where Keynote used to shine was in the animation and transitions available. They were more interesting, ran smoother (mainly due to the better hardware on which they ran) and generally looked a bit fancier. They also had an ace up their sleeve with an animation tool called "Magic Move," which makes certain animations a breeze—giving Keynote the upper hand for certain odds and ends. Ultimately, however, whizzy animation does not ensure a good presentation; indeed, most of the time, it makes for a truly awful one. But it was an advantage that Keynote had over it's nearest rival, PowerPoint.

As time has gone on, Microsoft developers have caught up and (horror) may have even overtaken Keynote on this as a result of PowerPoint's most recent releases.

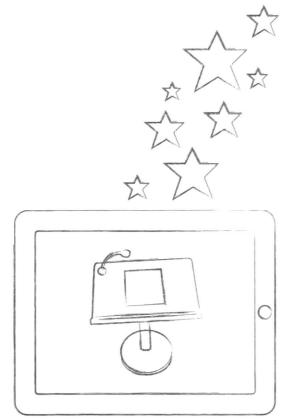

So, for want of a distinguishing feature, Keynote is a lot cheaper to buy. However, this is countered by the fact that the hardware it runs on is a lot more expensive than Windows computers. In short, the choice is yours.

What's not good?

In conjunction with the iPad, Keynote has done a great job getting Apple into the consciousness of today's tech savvy business presenter. Despite this, they don't seem to have made much investment in keeping Keynote ahead of the pack. The compatibility with PowerPoint remains patchy and still does not support many of the features people have come to expect from tablet solutions—most notably intelligent hyperlinking to support the interactive presentation requirements. This lack of investment has unwittingly led to a number of app providers exploiting the opportunity for a robust presentation app and aiding business presenters in their use of the iPad.

The other frustration is the Keynote iPad app's "lightness" versus its desktop equivalent; indeed, it is very much a slimmed down version. There is some logic behind this, as software developers recognize the fact that any tablet is imperfect when it comes to creating content. The lack of a permanent keyboard and mouse makes fine tuning content cumbersome and time consuming. However, there is a sense that the Keynote developers are happy to accept average rather than innovate to make the most out of the hardware the app sits on.

What they mix well with

In much the same way as PowerPoint acts as a foundation for repurposing presentations into different formats and media, Keynote has the option to share to PDF, printed formats, HTML, and QuickTime video.

Without a doubt, the biggest feather in its cap is its ability to work seamlessly on the iPad. For those business people who have made the move to a purely Apple environment (typically the creative sector and subject matter experts), this compatibility makes the switch from laptop to tablet to hard copy presentations a breeze.

Managed with care and consideration for each audience type, this has the potential to bring real power to your Blended Presenting strategy.

When to use it

In line with PowerPoint, Keynote works well for Formal presentations and for **linear** iPad presentations.

Ironically, Keynote's limitations come to the fore with *Interactive* presentations. The lack of custom show functionality means that building a presentation to support a truly interactive engagement can be a little clumsy and not particularly intuitive.

Keynote can also be useful when preparing for Informal presentations due to its ability to play on iPhones.

Who to use it with

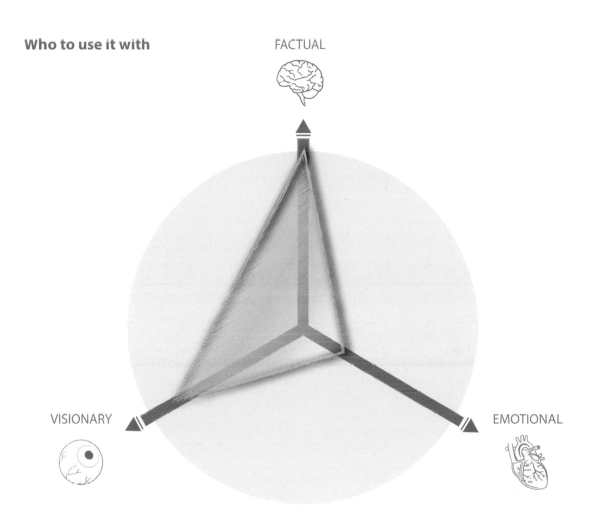

FACTUAL

VISIONARY

EMOTIONAL

How to use it

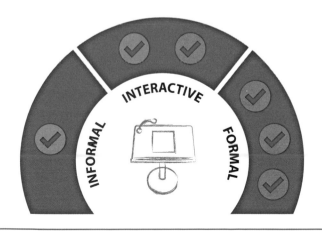

INTERACTIVE

INFORMAL

FORMAL

Prezi

If there's any slideware that demonstrates the market's hunger for new presentation approaches, it's Prezi. Prezi arrived in 2009 in a flurry of attention-grabbing PR and assurances that it would single-handedly change the face of presentations. And although it may have some way to go before knocking PowerPoint off the slideware top spot, it has forced many business presenters to completely revaluate the way they think about presentation visuals and delivery.

Prezi's secret weapon is the way it delivers information using its Zooming User Interface (ZUI). It has completely (and almost literally) turned the presentation experience on its head by allowing presenters to zoom and pan in and out of images, text, and other media. Because Prezi is based in the Cloud, it's cheap to work with (at the time of writing, the basic version is free to use) and accessible from any Internet-enabled piece of hardware. Subsequently, the novelty of this new approach coupled with a well-funded marketing campaign caused the number of registered Prezi users to skyrocket to over 18 million in 2012, and more than 250 million Prezi presentations were viewed online that year. It very quickly became a presentation *phenomenon*.

Prezi's refreshingly original visual approach makes it stand out from the multitude of standard linear presentation tools out there. However, there is a caveat—namely, the reports that sometimes, the Prezi experience is a little *too* extreme. Some audience members have experienced motion sickness–induced nausea when viewing fast action Prezi presentations on a large screen. And although some don't have as extreme a reaction, they're simply overwhelmed by the entire approach.

Perhaps because of its completely unique approach to visually delivering presentations, Prezi has divided many within the business presentations community.

Many people have embraced the slick transitions and new nonlinear approach to sharing their message; others have derided it as a one-trick pony that is more style than substance in terms of truly delivering a sticky, message-driven presentation.

My personal view is that Prezi has its place in the canon of presentation tools—*but* for a very specific type of engagement. To see it as a direct challenge to the likes of PowerPoint and Keynote is not only a bit naïve; it can be downright dangerous when presenting to certain audience types.

Let me explain.

What's good?

In addition to its unique and very clever zooming features, we must applaud Prezi for making business people think differently about their presentations. The software's very nature prevents presenters from mindlessly filling slide after slide with bullet points; more planning, pondering, and consideration of the audience is required before a presenter can develop the Prezi canvas. This is not to say that there are not bad, ill-conceived, and overly wordy Prezi presentations out there (!). It's just that this option makes it little more difficult to fall into the trap of creating autocue-type slides.

Perhaps Prezi's most obvious benefit is that it is so very different from the other options out there. You cannot underestimate the novelty factor when considering how to best engage your audience—and Prezi wholeheartedly delivers on this. However, bear in mind that this can be a double-edged sword.

If all your audience remembers is the cool zooming motion and doesn't take your message on board, the presentation will have been a failure. It's as simple as that.

What's not good?

Prezi is very good at one thing: zooming and panning. And that's pretty much as far as it goes. So if your presentation isn't going to benefit from this high-impact animated approach, Prezi probably isn't going to be much use.

Perhaps as a nod toward the greater functionality of tools like PowerPoint and Keynote, developers at Prezi are slowly increasing their tool's bells and whistles. For example, Prezi now offers fade animations and the ability to embed PowerPoint files. The ease by which presenters can import elements into Prezi is an important factor, as it remains extremely limited in it's ability to generate anything but the most basic shapes. In other words, pretty much everything needs to be created outside of Prezi and imported in, which can be both time consuming and frustrating. As a colleague said recently, "Man cannot live by zoom and pan alone."

Finally, there is no getting away from it; Prezi's unique zoom and pan functionality could very easily become an unwelcome distraction. In the most extreme cases, you might find sections of your audience turning a funny shade of green as you visually throw them across the screen one more time. But even in more moderate situations, you risk having them focus more on the transition than the *message*.

What they mix well with

Prezi works well as part of a Blended Presenting strategy. It's fairly intuitive to combine it with other technologies and approaches to engage an audience. It gives you just the right level of razzmatazz while keeping them on track and supporting your message.

It can be used alongside PowerPoint, converted to video (with a bit of jiggery pokery), and played as an introduction on the web or on an exhibition stand. In short, Prezi is probably best as part of an ensemble of presentation tools rather than sitting center stage for the vast majority of presentation scenarios.

You can think of it as a spice that you add to a meal to jazz it up. Used sparingly, it can enhance the meal and add real flavor and depth. Sprinkle it around too liberally and it will overpower the dish completely and leave a bad taste in the mouth. So use it with care!

When to use it

I'd hate to think that the plethora of caveats I issued in the previous paragraphs would lead you to shy away from trying Prezi and incorporating it into a Blended Presenting approach. The Prezi zoom and pan feature *does* lend itself to some pretty cool applications and can bring some much needed impact into the most intense and business-like presentations.

At Eyeful Presentations, we have used it most successfully to demonstrate a journey in several ways:

An animated timeline. This was particularly powerful when sharing an information technology (IT) road map or a company's historical experience in a quick and engaging way.

A process map. One of my favorite applications was when we took a business process outsource provider's prospect on a step-by-step journey to show them how the provider managed their cases.

A "fly through." We took visitors on a virtual tour of a large but highly secure warehouse facility for one of our logistics customers.

Prezi worked brilliantly for these very specific applications—but only these.

As with all the latest technology, it's about finding the right application for its cool widgets rather than blindly using them simply because they're new and different.

Who to use it with

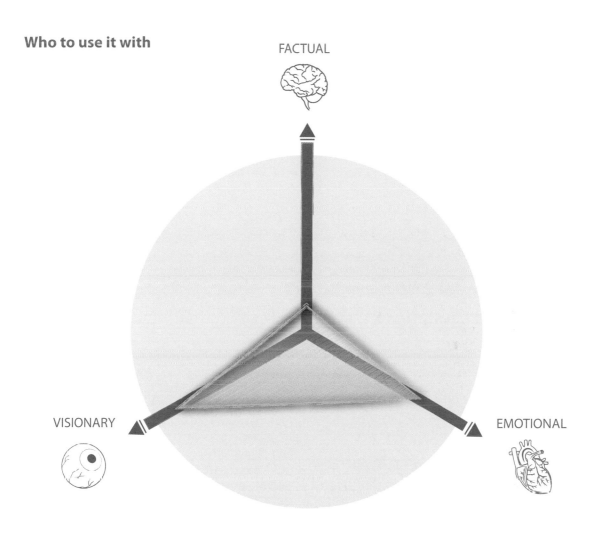

FACTUAL

VISIONARY

EMOTIONAL

How to use it

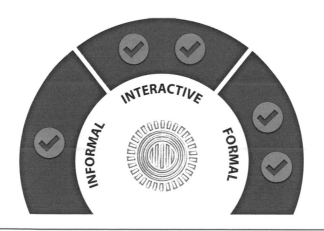

INTERACTIVE

INFORMAL

FORMAL

Whiteboard

The lowly whiteboard sits largely ignored in executive suites and meeting rooms in businesses of all sizes, across all parts of the world. They're occasionally dusted down, either to project a PowerPoint slide or Excel chart onto or for an enthusiastic product manager to leap into action and share their latest complex diagram with perplexed colleagues. If you look carefully enough, you'll see the faint remnants of the time someone used the wrong type of pen on the board, much to their own embarrassment and the chagrin of the premises supervisor. But most of the time, they just sit there unused, unloved, and underutilized, and representing a *huge* missed opportunity to business presenters everywhere.

When embraced, the whiteboarding concept unlocks a whole new level of interactivity with an audience. It allows presenters to engage in a completely different way to the more formal approaches.

The range of whiteboards available is vast—from the analogue versions which are simply a sheet of plastic mounted on the wall, to a fully digital version that links directly to your computer, is supported using pens/fingers/stylus, and has the ability to access the web, videos, and a host of other media. The joy with whiteboard presenting is that it really doesn't matter how technically advanced you or your audience are. This approach is about engaging your audience in the most pure way possible, with story, structure, and key visuals. And the fact that almost all businesses have a whiteboard—or, at worst, a paper flipchart in a conference room somewhere—means that you are never left without a medium by which to present.

What's good?

The simplicity of whiteboards is the secret to their success as a presentation tool. They represent a huge blank canvas upon which you can share your story, thereby allowing you to add the visual content when it supports your message—and leave other areas blank to complete in conjunction with your audience. Compared with the technical safety blanket that PowerPoint, Keynote, and the like provide, whiteboard presenting gently forces you to think and deliver visually—since writing up a series of bullet points on a vast whiteboard would seem more than a little, well, weird.

The whiteboard's very nature prompts discussion and interaction with your audience. It quickly becomes a collaborative experience, with all parties offering their thoughts and voicing their feelings.

Add to this the fact that they are available in pretty much every office the world over (and if you're struggling to find one, a pad of paper and pen works just fine for a small audience) and you're in good stead.

Even more powerful is the ability to **record the results** of you and your audience's combined efforts for posterity—either by hitting the screengrab button on electronic whiteboards or using your smartphone's camera to take a picture. You can then use this jointly produced masterpiece (with the audience's handwriting in place) as part of your post-presentation follow up—either as a proposal document, summary e-mail, or call to action reminder.

There's no denying it; being able to deliver your message in this way gives you some powerful choices.

It is powerfully disarming when you don't have to rely on the more traditional presentation tools. People automatically take notice, step away from their smartphones, and engage. And therein lies the power of whiteboard presenting as part of a Blended approach.

I recall visiting a huge global distribution company through our office in Holland to discuss their presentation development needs. It became obvious very early on in the meeting that we were one of a number of companies to whom they were speaking. Although this had been billed as an informal chat, they saw the meeting very much as a pitch.

As soon as my colleague and I sat down, they asked if we would like to connect a laptop to the projector on the desk, cooling down from the last vendor meeting. We responded by saying, maybe—but let's have a chat first so we could understand a little more about their requirements.

The audience was made up of three very senior people, short on time but big on vision—in terms of audience profile heat map, it was very one sided toward Visionary! As we discussed their business and the part presentations played (everything from multimillion Euro bids to internal comms presentations), we naturally gravitated toward the whiteboard. This allowed us to jointly build a model that established and sense-checked their needs and then, in a different color, applied these issues directly to the Eyeful Presentations model. The meeting went from a potential to a formal pitch to an engaging debate.

We won the business because we demonstrated that we not only understood their needs; we clarified and challenged them—and then **applied our model** to the situation to address them. And this only became possible because we put down the cursor and picked up a pen and then presented a structured story **that we knew intimately**.

What's not good?

Despite it's many benefits, whiteboard presenting is not without it's flaws.

A strong story is by far the most important element in making whiteboard presentations work. Without a strong story in place, the very thought of standing in front of a blank canvas will (quite naturally) bring on heart palpitations from the most experienced presenter.

Presenters, *especially* nervous ones, really need to know their story and be confident enough to respond and run with the audience's interactions while keeping everything on track. This increases the stakes exponentially—so approach with caution.

And although you *never* want to use PowerPoint and other slideware as an autocue, there is no doubt that a few choice pre designed words on a slide can help the nervous presenter stay on track. With insufficient knowledge or preparation, whiteboard presenting is the presentation equivalent of tightrope walking . . . without a safety net . . . over a ravine full of crocodiles.

The whiteboard approach also works only when the audience is willing to participate!

If they are in Formal mode and expect you to follow a specific agenda and format for the presentation, you run the risk of upsetting them by turning things on their head. Choose your moment, gauge your audience and know what you want to say before you attempt to say it.

What they mix well with

Whiteboard presenting works incredibly well as part of a blended approach. It might be to simplify some particularly technical information, work as an exercise to uncover an audience's needs and then align a solution accordingly—or simply serve to change the dynamics within the room.

When to use it

This model is normally best used as part of a mix, to be pulled out of the presentation toolkit at the point where audience engagement and buy-in is at it's most powerful. In my experience, this is rarely at the start or conclusion of your allotted speaking time; it's more likely to form the core of your presentation *Engage* stage.

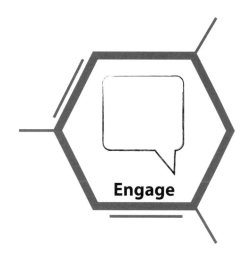

Who to use it with

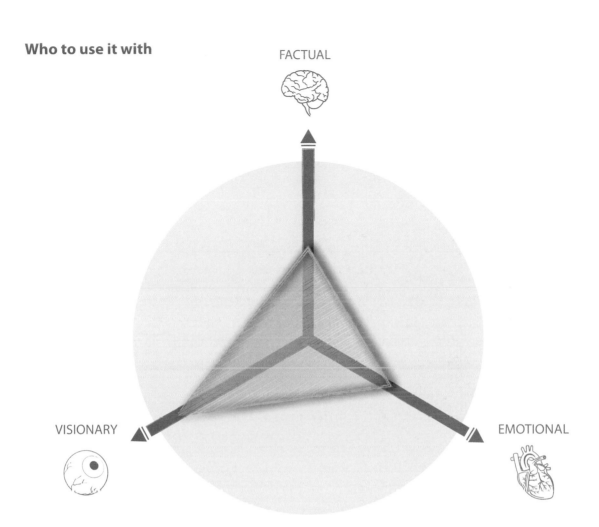

FACTUAL

VISIONARY

EMOTIONAL

How to use it

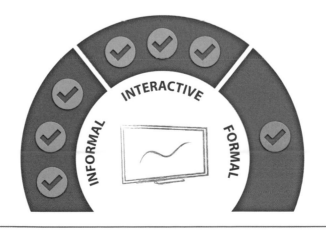

INTERACTIVE

INFORMAL

FORMAL

Hard Copy Document

On the surface, a hard copy presentation format shouldn't really be particularly noteworthy. Surely it's simply a static, printed version of PowerPoint or Keynote slides you'd typically associate with business presentations, right?

Actually, it's much more than that.

These presentations are beautifully bound, incredibly text heavy, and normally rather thick. Despite riding roughshod over pretty much every presentation rule known to man, certain sectors simply *love* them. It might be the vast amount of content that is shared in the very dense pages of text, that the velum coated covers appeal to the audience, or simply the "stackability" of the documents back at their offices. But financial services companies can't seem to get enough of them, investment companies adore them, and private equity houses go all of a quiver when they see them.

It really is all rather strange to me. And despite our regular protests, we at Eyeful Presentations have an array of customers who prefer to present in this format to this very specific audience type. Let's delve into why.

What's good?

This hybrid of document and presentation provides the audience with an almost word-for-word record of the meeting without automatically excluding the use of valuable visuals. The book's layout and construction, typically carried out in PowerPoint, makes it easy to use large, engaging imagery—so don't overlook this opportunity.

Additionally, the comprehensive nature of the content provides both presenter and audience with the confidence that all the information required will be in the document (somewhere!). Therefore, if audience members share the presentation with colleagues after the meeting, they're unlikely to misinterpret the message.

Despite my obvious frustration with this format of presentation, it is far more preferable to the scourge of many a meeting—the "slideument." *Slideument* is a made up word the venerable Garr Reynolds created to describe the awful mess that ensues when a slide presentation is made too wordy to work as a visual tool but not wordy enough to act as a document. The compromise fails on both sides.

As an aside, there is a way of creating an aesthetically pleasing hard copy presentation from visual PowerPoint/Keynote slides by using the Notes section of each software package.* This often overlooked feature within the software gives you the option to format the layout of your speaker notes in such a way that, when printed, the finished document not only contains the strong visuals you used to present, but also the copious amount of copy required for such a presentation.

*Hats off to friend and fellow presentation geek, @NolanHaims for spreading the word on this approach and subsequently saving the sanity of scores of audience members across the world.

What's not good?

The biggest issue with hard copy presentations is the constant debate over whether it's a presentation or a visual document. Presenting from a visual document is downright difficult, since it can cause you to fall into the trap of reading large sections of the content to your audience (something you tend to do even more when you're nervous).

As such, it is very easy for the presentation to actually form a barrier between the presenter and the audience—which is, of course, the polar opposite of your objective. Building a rapport and engaging an audience is best managed through a shared experience, something that the hard copy document's binary approach does little to support.

What they mix well with

The saving grace of the hard copy presentation is that it is **invaluable** as a post presentation follow-up tool.

Packed schedules and the chaos of everyday business life means that you won't always get to deliver your presentation to absolutely everyone who needs to hear it. It might be that one of the key decision makers for a sales presentation was unable to attend and relies on colleagues to interpret your message. It might be that an internal audience will want to ponder on your recommendations before acting on them. In these situations, the follow-up hard copy presentation is priceless.

When to use it

Hard copy presentations are best saved as a follow-up tool to help reaffirm your message, especially if key stakeholders have been unable to attend your face-to-face meeting.

You can also use them for the very specific financial audiences previously mentioned, or when a more conventional approach is appropriate. (This is a polite way of saying that if your audience simply will not accept another approach, you must follow this in deference to them.)

Who to use it with

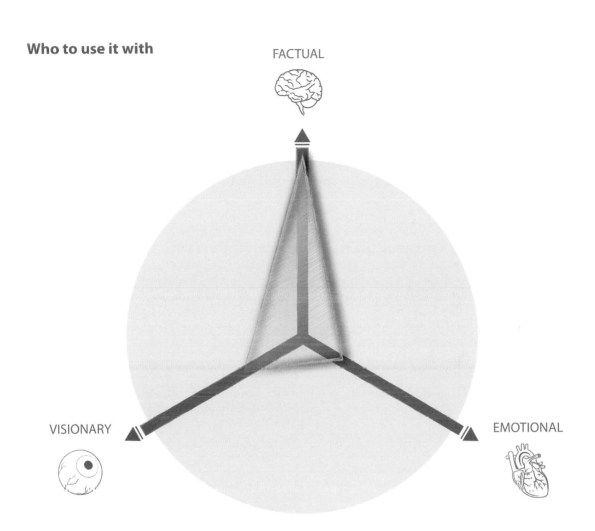

FACTUAL

VISIONARY

EMOTIONAL

How to use it

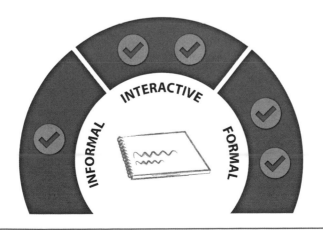

INTERACTIVE

INFORMAL

FORMAL

So how does this plethora of presentation scenarios, tools, and styles play out in real-life? How easy is it to use the concept of Blended Presenting in a situation such as a sales presentation? By way of answering that, I share the following story.

I recall working with a company in the United Kingdom that had a real problem with their presentation. The relationship began when they tried to sell me human resources (HR) services for our fast-growing company.

It wasn't particularly their salesperson; she was well presented, obviously knew her content, was proud of her product, and had run a good meeting up to a point.

It wasn't particularly their slide deck either (although this was incredibly corporate and a little too uptight for its own good).

And it wasn't their message. They had a good product and a relatively clear point about the impact their offering would have on our business.

The problem was the way the salesperson *handled* the presentation. Up until the moment she fired up her laptop, we'd been getting on well. She'd done a fine job in building rapport, had obviously done her research on our business, asked me sensible and educated questions, and answered all my queries clearly and confidently.

However, as soon as she entered "presentation mode," she transformed from a warm professional in whom I had faith into a robot. Over the course of 20 minutes and far too many slides to count, she slowly removed all sense of credibility from herself *and* her employer.

I asked her why she felt the need to deliver a PowerPoint presentation at that stage of the meeting. As a prospect, I was warmed up and ready to do a deal—full of positive energy; sentiment she then killed by unveiling and delivering the living embodiment of death by PowerPoint.

Her answer shocked me: "Our Sales Director says we have to deliver this PowerPoint presentation every time, in exactly this order and using this exact script."

It transpired that the company had worked with a presentation design company who had convinced them that the best way to get their message across was to deliver their story, word-for-word *without any deviation*. That, coupled with the Sales Director's lack of confidence in the sales force, had turned a good proposition into a complete turn-off within minutes.

This lack of presentation flexibility is occurring across the globe every minute of every day. It's costing sales people the opportunity to close deals. It's costing marketing people reputation—and most important, it's costing audiences time and, I'm sure in some cases, their mental health!

And Now the Good News . . .

By taking a Blended approach to the same proposition, we are able to slim down the vast number of slides required in the company PowerPoint and offer more visual ways of demonstrating key points, be that via the slide deck or on a whiteboard or a pad of paper and ultimately free the sales team to do what it did best: communicate and sell.

Blended Presenting has that power, and the Presentation Lab "experiments" in the next section will demonstrate just how.

The Salesperson Checklist

- ☑ Do research
- ☑ Be prompt
- ☑ Make good first impression
- ☑ Build rapport
- ☑ Answer queries confidently
- ☑ Get client on verge of signing
- ☑ Produce the presentation

- ☑ Ruin atmosphere
- ☑ Keep to the script
- ☑ Nudge client back awake
- ☑ Bumble through slides
- ☑ Lose client
- ☑ Leave politely
- ☑ Repeat

THE PRESENTATION LAB

Putting the Theory into Practice

F

Element   A B C D E **F** G H

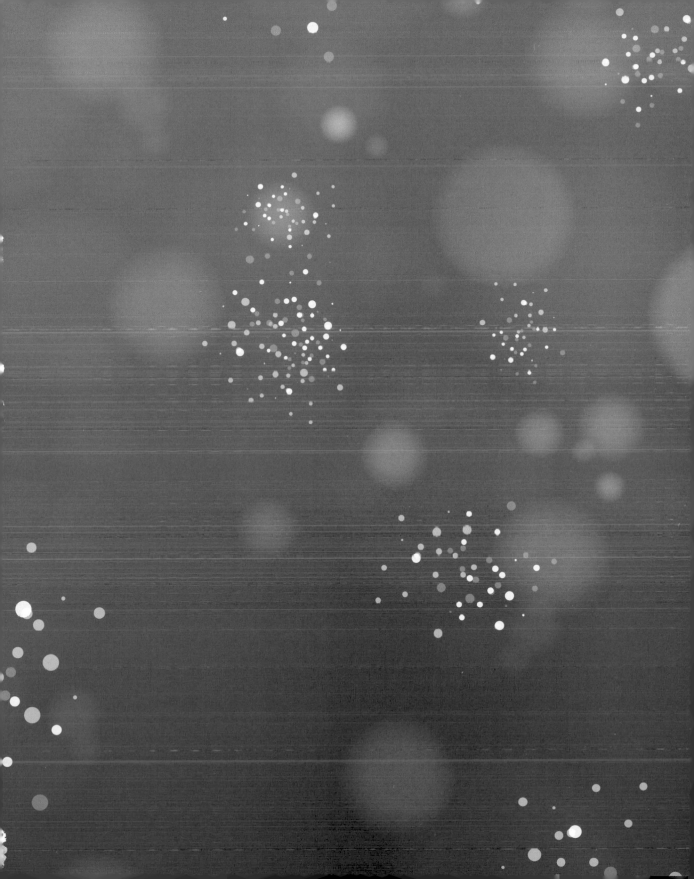

Putting the Theory into Practice

F₁

Element   A B C D E **F** G H

The Presentation Optimization process has been developed over many years, and as the result of creating literally thousands of presentations. It works.

However, no matter how carefully we've crafted the sections of this book, there's no getting away from the fact that the real impact of the process only comes to light when you see it working in real life scenarios. So before you get to the real excitement of witnessing this with your own business, you'll see it play out in this section's detailed examples.

Each of the following case studies is based on projects that the team at my company, Eyeful Presentations, has worked on. Not only have they been chosen to represent the wide array of presentation formats that business people across the globe use every day, but they also highlight some of the more challenging scenarios in which presenters find themselves. From the "win at all costs" pitch to dealing with the tightrope of sharing bad news within a business, presentations bring with them huge pressure and responsibility. For this reason, we have chosen to make these case studies anonymous. Quite simply, the more we are able to share in terms of backstory and real-life issues, the more value they will bring you and your organization's next project.

These case studies will demonstrate how the Presentation Optimization process provides a reassuring structure around which to build and sense check your message development as well as your choice of content, visuals, and tools used. No presentation is ever the same, yet each project shares the assurance and confidence that comes from applying a belt and braces approach to their development.

Stepping up in front of an audience, safe in the knowledge that you have a strong and well reasoned story to tell is strangely empowering.

So with this in mind, let's stop talking about presentations and let's start sharing some real-life examples.

Case Study 1
The Bid Presentation

Stakes and emotions run high with bid presentations. They typically represent the final hurdle that you and your bid team have to negotiate before a procurement team awards a contract. Prior to this, you will have slaved away for hours preparing a response to their invitation to tender (ITT in procurement speak) and then spent the intervening time wringing your hands and pacing the room. Tensions are high.

The good news is that being asked to present your bid submission means you're still in the game. The bad news is that the decision that could (possibly) bring you and your business untold riches comes down to how well you and the bid team perform in front of the audience. No pressure, then.

Our client: Medium-sized manufacturing business

The presenter(s): CEO

Their audience: Category managers and procurement team from large national retailer

The backstory: This company's CEO approached us because he was facing his biggest challenge to date. After many happy years of supporting a large national retailer with a range of products, the organization had been informed that the retailer was undergoing a procurement exercise to rationalize the supply base from over 50 down to three main suppliers.

Our client's immediate reaction was one of horror and disappointment. Horror because losing this contract would mean huge job redundancies across the business (his rough estimate was up to 80 percent of the long-serving workforce) and disappointment because the strong relationship he and his predecessor had developed over many years was apparently worthless.

After a period of blind panic and the collation of vast amounts of information to demonstrate how valuable their products, skills and experience were to the retailer, the CEO reached out to us to work on his PowerPoint slides.

Following a full and frank discussion regarding the situation, we recommended reworking the PowerPoint presentation by employing the Presentation Optimization methodology to bring greater focus to the message and align it directly to this important audience.

Stage 1
Analyzing the audience

The audience was composed of a mixture of disciplines, from the impartial procurement team to the category managers who had built a trusted relationship with our client. Despite their different backgrounds and experience with our client, it became clear very quickly that they shared the same objective: to get the best value for their customers by improving the price points while maintaining their impeccable reputation as a retailer who provided great quality.

As the heat map demonstrates, the factual element of the audience held much, but not all, of the influence in the room. We had to ensure that all present clearly understood the message on cost savings; however, we also needed to address the considerable pull of the Visionary element. Indeed, it was agreed at the workshop stage that creating a hardnosed, cost-saving presentation would have alienated those elements of the audience that wanted to look beyond the new contract's financial benefits.

Importantly, the CEO felt strongly that the relationship going forward had to reflect the value of trust and innovation that they brought to the table. If it was purely about the money, it was probably not a contract they wanted to win.

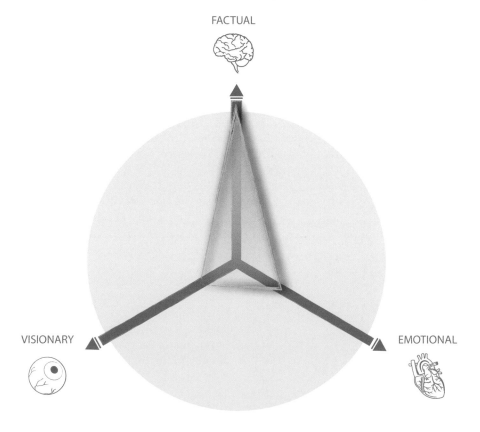

FACTUAL

VISIONARY

EMOTIONAL

Stage 2
Defining the message

Without doubt, this was the most important stage of the entire Presentation Optimization process for this project. There was no lack of information; our client had more than 300 pages of notes, ideas, and reference material. However, for all the passion and enthusiasm, it lacked focus and a simple takeaway message for the audience to grasp.

What followed was an intense workshop session aimed at both filtering this copious information into relevant groups and then directly challenging the concepts being put forward by asking questions like:

- So what if our client had a research and development (R&D) team to develop new products—why was this of value to our audience?

- So what if they had the best customer satisfaction results in their sector—why was this of value to our audience?

- So what if they had won awards for their management of sustainable products—how was this of value to our audience?

(Are you sensing a pattern?)

By challenging the value behind each of our client's bold claims, we were able to build up a much better picture of how they could play these back to address the retailer's main concerns: value and quality.

Once these building blocks were in place, we were able to sort them into a simple Need Creation structure using our storyflow process:

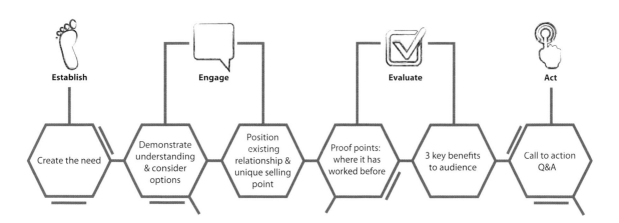

Stage 3
Collating the content

With the structure in place, it was time to filter the content to identify the key points to add to the presentation. By thinking in headline form, we were able to create clear content that locked together to help demonstrate and support the strong overarching message.

At this point, we decided on a two-pronged approach in terms of presentation materials. We would create an extremely visual PowerPoint presentation to frame the general proposition as well as play to the strong Visionary element within the audience. We would then supplement this with a more Factual hard copy document, which we'd refer to at key points within the presentation, demonstrating pricing rationale or projected cost savings.

This enabled us to ensure that all valuable content was available to the audience in a format that was easily accessible when required.

Stage 4
Valuable visuals

Despite our initial fears of him wanting to use the PowerPoint slides as an autocue, the CEO was happy to present using very visual slides. This confidence came from his knowledge of the subject, coupled with access to a strong logical structure to follow and presentation tools that covered both the 'big picture' elements as well as the bid detail.

This approach allowed us to play upon the visual subtext behind some of the imagery. Rather than simply showing products in situ, we built upon the retailer's brand positioning as a store people visit to improve their homes and their family time together. The visuals subtly moved the bid presentation from being purely about unit costs of different product lines into a discussion about how the partnership between both parties would further enhance the retailer's position in the marketplace.

Stage 5
Delivery

We spent a couple of days supporting and coaching the CEO before the big day. This included ensuring his complete confidence in the presentation story and flow, understanding the importance of pace, and understanding how to use a Blended Presenting approach to get the most out of both the PowerPoint and hard copy presentation.

The outcome

The presentation went like a dream. Our strategies to maximize engagement with the different elements of the audience worked well and quickly took the form of an interactive conversation. This enabled all parties to test their understanding and truly get under the skin of our client's proposition.

Our client not only retained the existing line of business but also expanded into other areas with the retailer. This safeguarded the jobs of more than 100 people in their manufacturing plant and heralded the start of a new chapter for the business.

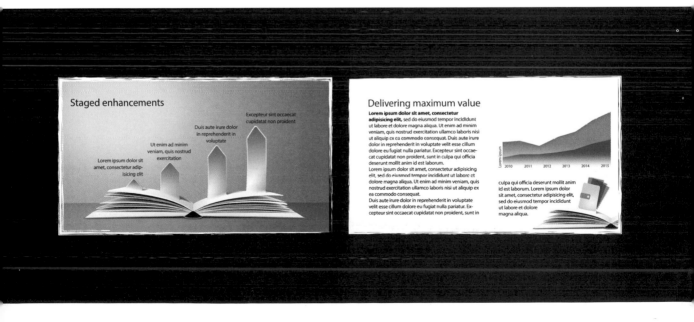

Case Study 2
The Conference Presentation

Conference presentations pose a wonderful dilemma to the presenter. Of course, they provide a wonderful opportunity for your story to engage and resonate with a large audience. However, they also put your entire presentation in danger of being hampered by a number of limiting factors out of your control. In the wrong hands or without due preparation, elements such as technology, previous speakers, and your position in the agenda can directly affect your presentation's effectiveness.

The inevitable profile that comes with speaking at a conference can often be the catalyst for a range of anxieties: Will I lose my train of thought halfway through? Will people simply switch off if I'm not immediately engaging? Should I start with a joke? What happens if I fall over when walking onto the stage? The list of potential conference presentation maladies is almost endless. But without doubt, the biggest source of stress is lack of considered planning and development up front.

The good news is that this is easy to fix.

Our client: Large Commercial Bank

The presenter(s): SVP of Commercial Strategy

Their audience: Conference delegates from the largest accountancy body in the United Kingdom

The backstory: The very senior contact within the bank was a little nervous; he'd been asked to provide the concluding presentation at a prestigious event for one of the most respected institutes in the country. Not only was the audience made up of very influential individuals, but the newly promoted SVP was a particularly anxious presenter. This fear was made all the more paralyzing thanks to a widely reported, poorly received presentation that had taken place earlier that year to a gathering of peers at a banking event. Needless to say, the pressure was on.

Our client's previous conference presentations had been prepared for him by his public relations (PR) agency. In light of the global banking crisis that had been particularly hard felt in the United Kingdom, the topic for this forthcoming event, The Role of the Banking Sector in Turning around the British Economy, was contentious—and proving a difficult one for the PR agency to shape. In frustration, our client's personal assistant contacted us and asked for assistance.

After a full review of the far-reaching and potentially incendiary topic and the available content, we agreed that a strong story structure was required to navigate through some of the inevitably negative preconceptions within the auditorium.

Stage 1
Analyzing the audience

In light of the tricky relationship between the banks and business following the global financial crisis, a good understanding of the audience profile was absolutely vital in ensuring that our client communicated the message in a way that allowed it to be heard. The audience was made up of financially astute people whose customers, friends, and family had been impacted in some way by the crisis; in many ways, they were looking for someone to blame. As such, the audience heat map was identified as follows:

Ultimately it was important to recognize how normally Factual thinkers in the audience had become incredibly Emotionally charged—and then develop a presentation message that addressed this. It was equally crucial for our client to address the need of the Visionary element of the audience and navigate their way through the detail that had the potential to alienate listeners.

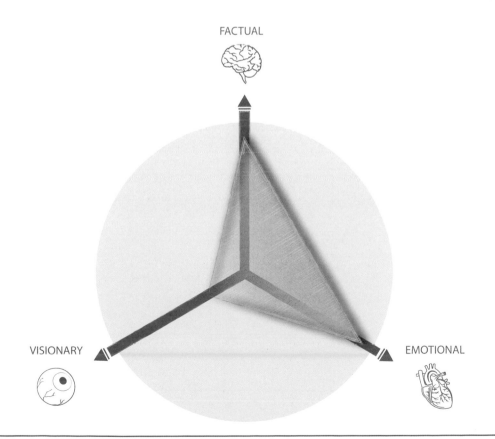

FACTUAL

VISIONARY

EMOTIONAL

Stage 2
Defining the message

As is often the case with particularly senior contacts, the speaker's availability was extremely limited. Therefore, the workshop process we normally employed for such a project was simply not logistically possible. We would need to develop the messaging remotely and review it periodically through online meetings.

We commenced by reviewing the vast amount of data the client and PR agency provided. As key categories of information emerged, we ordered and tested them to provide a very high-level story and structure for the client to review.

One strong message emerged through the process. Using the storyflow format as a basis for a series of review discussions, all parties were able to quickly identify with this key message. They could then offer ideas and supporting data to shape how to share it with this profile of audience.

The story structure evolved over time, from a conventional conference approach:

• Tell them what you're going to tell them

• Tell them

• Tell them what you've told them

. . . to a more controlled and structured approach using a "Specific Message Headline" model. We agreed this approach would allow the speaker to address the audience's specific concerns head-on.

With the key message and story structure identified, it was time to move on to the *Content* phase.

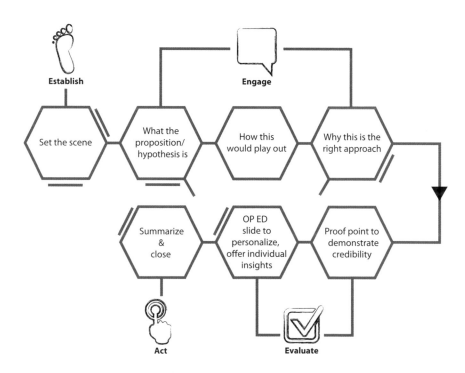

Stage 3
Collating the content

Given the lack of access to the client to run a traditional Presentation Optimization workshop, the message development had started very much in the content detail. As such, the process was one step ahead when it came to agreeing on which elements of the content were important to retain and which ones were left on the cutting room floor.

Previously, the words *banking* and *conference* would immediately conjure up images of slides densely populated with charts and data. This analytical approach was always seen as a quick way of establishing credibility, despite the fact that it frequently created a barrier between the audience and the presenter. This project's strong message—combined with the unusual audience profile—allowed us to think beyond merely quoting a series of statistics. Everyone realized that the content needed to address the strong Emotional charge within the room, so we combined data and statistics with softer anecdotal evidence to support the key message.

Stage 4
Valuable visuals

This different approach opened up a variety of options for the presentation's visual element. We recognized that the audience would have spent the better part of the day being bombarded with charts and graphs, and attention spans were likely to be suffering as a result.

With this in mind, we introduced elements of animation into the slide deck at key stages. These subtle graphics brought charts to life in line with key points, while more creative animations signposted the move from one section of the presentation to the next. The animations were not designed to distract; however, we recognized that the use of some motion would come as a welcome break to an audience who had been inundated with dry slides all day.

Most important, combining anecdotal evidence with a story-based structure allowed us to use imagery that exploited visual subtext. Powerful images of the banking crisis' impact—from redundant employees walking out of offices with cardboard boxes full of their desk clutter, to pictures of empty and decaying commercial premises—had a noticeable effect on the audience.

The bank's acceptance that the crisis had had far-reaching consequences was powerful and disarming. Importantly, it also provided a stage upon which to deliver the presentation's key message: that the banking community needed to play a key role in rebuilding the economy.

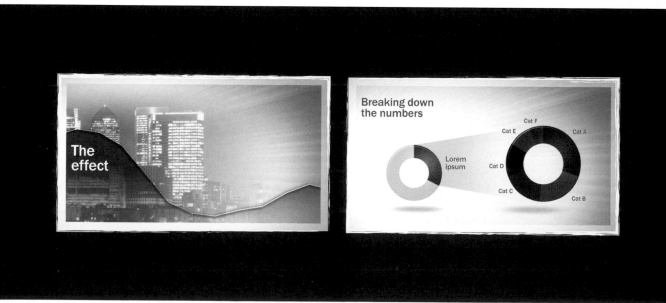

Stage 5
Delivery

The very nature of a large industry conference means that most presenters opt to use slideware like PowerPoint or Keynote, and our client was no different. Although they recognized the value of engaging the audience with other tools such as Prezi or large-scale whiteboarding, they were keen to deliver a presentation in a format that didn't "rock the boat."

The stakes were high, and in light of some of the difficulties the client had experienced at previous conferences, they understandably wanted to play it safe. Indeed, such was their concern regarding this event that they also commissioned us to write the complete script, word for word, which would then be delivered to the presenter via autocue.

The outcome

The presentation was well received by the audience and the press who recognized a new level of transparency in the messaging. It also elevated our client's profile within his own bank, allowing others to see the value of investing time in developing a structured and fully considered presentation from a blank piece of paper rather than simply summarizing vast amounts of data and other content.

Case Study 3
The Sales Presentation

Sales presentations come in all shapes and sizes, from the ubiquitous laptop PowerPoint deck that forms the most important part of a salesperson's arsenal to newer tablet-based solutions and other visual tools. Whatever the format and whatever the product or service they are designed to help sell, one thing is guaranteed: There are a lot of them!

Of all the presentation forms, the sales presentation is possibly the most hotly debated within a business. The sales force (understandably) sees it as their tool; marketing folks see it as a piece of branded collateral and the product team members are anxious to ensure it has the most up-to-date information in place. Add to that opinion and influence from the legal team and the CEO, and you have the perfect storm. This one of the main reasons most sales presentations fail at delivering their objective; rather than providing a clear and structured argument for buying, they stumble around between braggadocio and confusing the audience with overly complex facts, figures, and product features.

Ultimately, sales presentations need to be led by their intended audience's needs, not by bickering internal teams. A prospect-focused sales presentation is an incredibly powerful tool in the right hands. If you can get it right, your proposition becomes understandable, engaging and with a strong call to action, in other words, just what the sales doctor ordered.

Our client: Multinational finance provider

The presenter(s): Global sales team

Their audience: Brand and Category managers for high-profile global brands

The backstory: We had a long-standing relationship with this customer and had worked on a variety of conference and internal presentations for them. The relationship had built to the point that the global HQ had started to engage us on much higher profile projects, culminating in a complete overhaul of a major sales PowerPoint deck.

The sales management had voiced their concerns that their existing presentation was more of a hindrance than a help in most meetings. They felt it did little to build a relationship with the prospect, and it had been created in isolation by the marketing team. As a result, many members of the sales team were either creating their own versions of the presentation or ditching it completely and, in their own words, winging it. Clearly, something had to change.

A quick review of the existing deck made the issues abundantly apparent: It was packed to the rafters with data, statistics, and legal caveats that did little to build need or instill confidence for the prospect. Equally, the very generic slides left the audience feeling that they were on the receiving end of a "canned" presentation. This would be bad enough news for small-value business, but as each of these deals were typically $2.5 to $5 million in value, it was quickly becoming a major issue.

The obvious first move was to pull all the internal customer stakeholders together and run them through a Presentation Optimization process to define a clear and valuable message—and then build content accordingly.

Stage 1
Analyzing the audience

Our customer was fortunate to work with some very high-profile brands' marketing and financial teams. Without doubt, the audience's marketing segment had a reputation as thought leaders in their field, both in terms of managing brands and developing customer engagement campaigns. On first impressions, some of them may have come across as aloof; others simply wore the confidence of people who knew they were very good at their job, yet they were also looking for new ideas and inspiration. As a result, there was a high Visionary element within the audience.

However, this Visionary element was countered to a certain extent by a strong Factual pull from the business's financial elements. Although looking to extend or challenge brand perceptions with innovative campaigns, there was a strong underlying sense that our client had to demonstrate a return on investment (ROI) before budgets were approved.

These two strong elements within a typical audience for our customer led us to identify the heat map as follows:

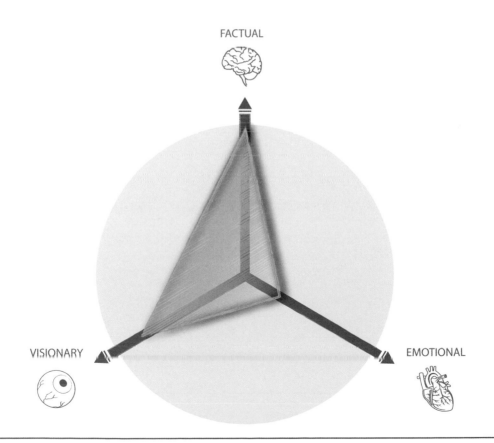

FACTUAL

VISIONARY

EMOTIONAL

Stage 2
Defining the message

Developing the message was a relatively straightforward process. As is often the case, once all parties started to discuss their understanding of the customer issues, they reached consensus remarkably quickly!

To aid the process, the consultant decided not to aim for one "killer message" and instead look to develop the presentation around three key messages that would resonate across the diverse audience profile. This also allowed the workshop participants to debate the merits of a range of messages rather than fiercely protect their own standpoint.

Perhaps the biggest challenge was the major overhaul to the presentation's structure. We were looking not only to extend the format beyond simply PowerPoint but to also include hard copy and iPad versions. We dramatically changed the functionality across the slide deck.

By moving away from a standard linear presentation to a more interactive toolkit approach, we had compelled the presenters to engage the audience in a more intimate and conversational style. The new structure allowed them to drill-down to information and examples in response to their customers' interest rather than working from slide to slide in a lecture style. This not only broke down the barriers but also allowed the presenter to respond to questions in a much more natural but authoritative way.

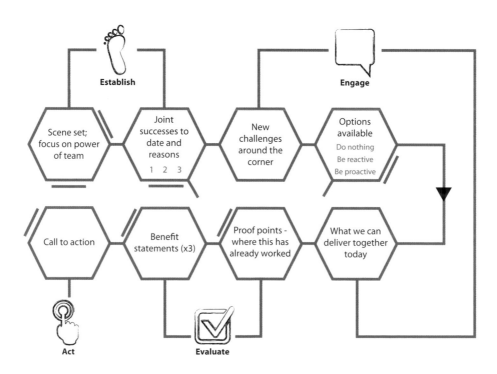

Stage 3
Collating the content

There was a vast amount of content to wade through. Following the workshop session to develop the message and high level structure, the consultant offered a presentation amnesty to all parties involved. The thinking was simple—there would be small nuggets of gold within the plethora of PowerPoint slides used by different parts of the global team that would support the three key messages.

Most important, the new format and story structure allowed us to challenge the status quo. We were able to lose many of the text-heavy slides and consolidate the detailed content as a leave-behind hard copy deck. Additionally, the new interactive format allowed us to push the company credentials element to the back of the presentation. As a result, the audience was greeted with content that applied to their issues rather than a long list extolling our customer's virtues and achievements.

Stage 4
Valuable visuals

The project quickly picked up the pace, and many people saw it as an opportunity to ditch the bullet points and embrace a much more visual approach. That said, we took care not to alienate the wide range of presenters who would be using this tool; some had felt comforted by having some text on the slide.

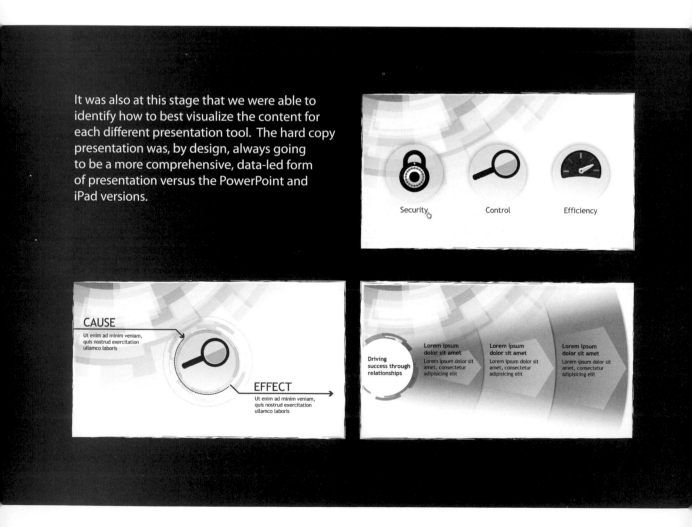

It was also at this stage that we were able to identify how to best visualize the content for each different presentation tool. The hard copy presentation was, by design, always going to be a more comprehensive, data-led form of presentation versus the PowerPoint and iPad versions.

Stage 5
Delivery

Coaching presenters on how to use these new presentation tools to maximum effect was an important part of the roll-out. It helped ensure that they would embrace the new sales tools rather than view them with suspicion. Uptake of the new approach was a key measure of success; we would have failed if the mavericks within the sales team had continued to take their own path in front of prospects.

It was also important that the team personalized each of the presentations before delivering them to a prospect. This went beyond simply adding a company logo to the front slide; it required the sales team to properly research the prospect, adding relevant information within the deck to demonstrate understanding and synergy.

The outcome

It's fair to say that the new presentation's very different approach and format took some 'bedding in' with a few isolated groups within the sales team. Thankfully, the management team's support and belief played a crucial part in ensuring that the few remaining rebels were coached into understanding the new approach's benefits. We were able to support this through a series of online coaching and technical training sessions.

Overall, the new format and tool options have been a huge hit with prospects and presenters. Audiences have commented on the flexibility of the presentation—"We feel like we're being listened to" while presenters have embraced the flexibility it provides them in front of their prospect.

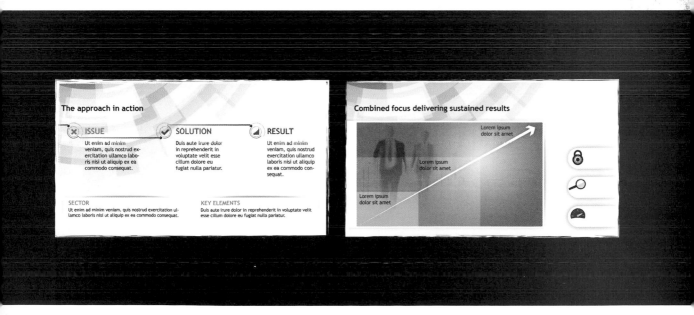

Case Study 4
The Internal Presentation

Internal communication is a tricky thing to get right.

Frequently, important internal messages get lost in the noise of everyday work life—often, ironically, as a result of the large amounts of internal communication, formal and informal. Countless companywide e-mails, intranet postings, and internal meetings all add to the noise, much of which is either irrelevant to the majority of people or quickly pulled together in an ad hoc way.

The internal presentation is a great example of the good and bad elements within in-company communication. The intention is normally good—"We have some important information that we need to share with our employee team"—possibly related to the company's financial performance, new strategies or acquisitions. However, for all these good intentions, most internal presentations fail in the key elements: audience engagement, clear and focused messages, relevant content, and engaging visuals. There is often a sense that internal presentations can be a little shabby around the edges because external audiences won't be viewing the slides. It's as if its 'internal presentation' status gives the presenter license to cut a few corners—when this couldn't be further from the truth.

In fact, internal presentations are often the most important and influential presentations many of us will ever make. Clear and engaging internal presentations can help turn a failing business around, engage an employee team and celebrate success in the most inclusive way. Failing to invest sufficient time and energy in such a communication is failing to invest in your company and its people. Internal presentations really are that important.

Our client: Multinational IT Services Group

The presenter(s): Chairman

Their audience: Heads of Business Units (Global)

The backstory: We were called in by the customer at the last moment to try and bring an incredibly important internal presentation to life. The Chairman and the board had to communicate the rationale behind a new global strategy that included a number of contentious but important changes—far-reaching changes that would directly impact a large proportion of the global workforce. As a result, the news of the revised strategy had been a closely guarded secret, with only a handful of top executives aware of any changes afoot.

The small internal team responsible for coordinating the communication had wrestled with the best way to share it across the business. They'd considered a number of ideas, including a company-wide videoconference or distribution of a detailed document. They ultimately decided that the Chairman would deliver a presentation to his senior board on the changes. Then the senior team would use this same presentation to disseminate the information within their divisions through a series of face-to-face meetings.

It was at this point that we were called in.

Stage 1
Analyzing the audience

As is often the case with internal presentations about big change, the normal nature of the audience changes quite dramatically when there is a perceived threat to their security. As with every large business, the workforce would normally be made up of a mix of Factual, Emotional, and Visionary profiles. This mix would flex in line with the presentation type, from being on the receiving end of a sales pitch or listening to a company update.

Naturally, a large-scale strategic change was going to push the audience very heavily toward the Emotional behaviors. It was crucial to factor in not just the immediate Emotional response but also the subsequent questions that would come later in the process. A key measure of success was that the audience understood and was engaged with all the information shared—and didn't go off on an anxiety-fuelled tangent.

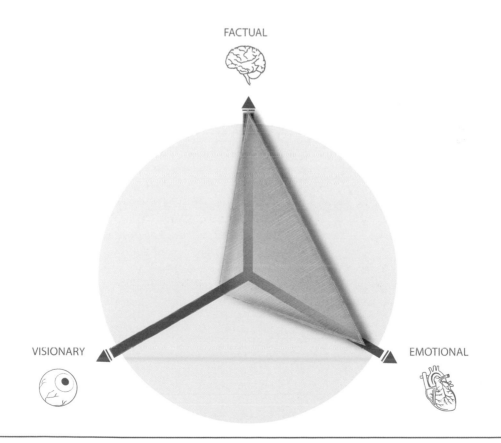

FACTUAL

VISIONARY

EMOTIONAL

Stage 2
Defining the message

The message was so much more than job losses. The strategic changes were about protecting the business, maintaining competitive advantage and addressing new threats. However the post-presentation water cooler conversation topic was doubtlessly going to be about people's job security. We knew we had to meticulously plan the story's structure to ensure that all the points were covered and understood.

After much discussion with the Chairman and his team, we recommended keeping the presentation as short and focused as possible. There was no benefit in overloading the audience with too much information; the structure needed to provide the presenters with the opportunity to quickly put the changes in context and then cut to the chase as to what this meant to the people in the audience. We were determined to make this the most audience-centric internal presentation the company had ever delivered.

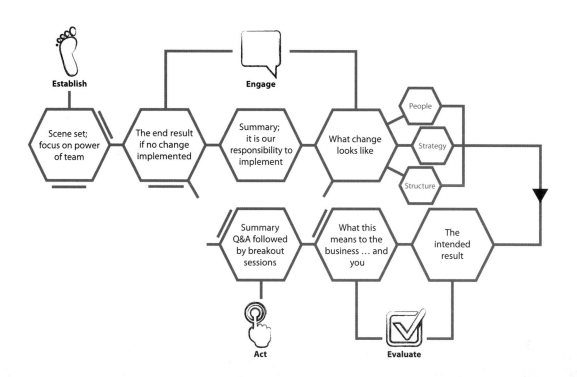

Stage 3
Collating the content

Naturally, a change of this magnitude was based on a vast amount of data and reasoning. No matter how devastating for those impacted by the job losses, the new strategic approach was absolutely necessary to address the coming challenges in the marketplace—and the customer had the content to prove it.

However, we took the view that the inevitable Emotional response from the audience would render much of the available content almost useless. At best, they'd ignore it—and possibly even misconstrue it.

We therefore recommended a Blended presenting approach to the communication. First, share the Executive Summary version of the new strategy (including the contentious elements) with the audiences face to face. This was to be supported with a much more detailed hard copy document, which the speaker would refer to throughout the presentation, highlighting areas for audience members to review post presentation. A series of Q&A sessions were then scheduled to coincide with the introduction of the HR function within each of the divisions.

Stage 4
Valuable visuals

The nature of the material being presented plus the addition of a text heavy hard copy support document meant that we were keen to make the slides as visual as we possibly could. The development of simple visuals to illustrate the changes and their intended impact was designed to enable audience members to engage with the message, despite their attentions probably being elsewhere.

Interestingly, we recognized that the strong Emotional audience profile meant that using images with powerful visual subtext was less important than a typical presentation. The subject matter ensured that they were already emotionally engaged.

The development of visuals for the hard copy presentation was also relatively subdued. The purpose of the document was to share sufficient detail and content to support the main story, and it was designed to make navigation as simple as possible.

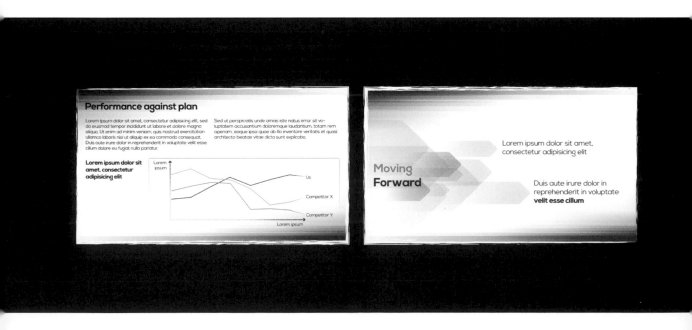

Putting the Theory into Practice

Stage 5
Delivery

The presentation was going to be cascaded throughout the business, from the Chairman down through his direct reports and divisional heads. Its sensitive nature, coupled with a wide variety of presenters, prompted a series of coaching sessions run across three different locations.

There is undoubtedly an art to delivering an emotionally charged message using the Blended Presenting method. So we took time to ensure all parties were comfortable and completely prepared before making the announcement.

The outcome

Despite the difficult subject matter, the presentation and communication process was regarded as a success by all involved in the project. The clarity of the message ensured that all affected parties were aware of just how the changes would affect them and the next actions to take. This addressed any potential false information from being spread across and then outside the business (Think of the game telephone.)

The company remains a major player in their sector and has managed to stay strong and relevant through tough economic times.

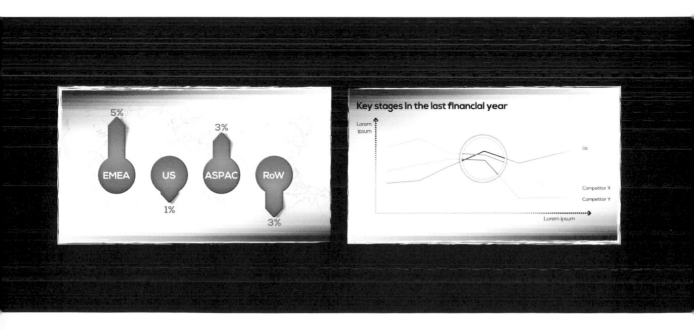

In Case of Emergency . . . Strategies for Dealing with Last Minute Deadlines

G

Element   A B C D E F **G** H

As with so many other areas in life, sometimes presentation plans and intentions go awry. Things beyond your control kind of get in the way and hijack your best intentions.

It might be a colleague who falls sick just before the big pitch, relying on you to jump to the rescue and deliver the presentation. Or maybe your kindly boss lets you know at the last minute that he or she would like you to present your thoughts on a particular topic at the next board meeting . . . which is in two days. Heck, it might be as the result of reading this book a few days ahead of an important presentation and realizing what you'd developed simply isn't up to scratch. (If this is the case, apologies. But it's for your own good!)

Whatever the reason for running around the office with an anxious look upon your face muttering "audience heat map" or "visual subtext" to yourself, panic not. Here are some strategies for dealing with the little presentation curve balls life occasionally throws at you.

Note: Each strategy assumes that you will be presenting using visuals, courtesy of something like PowerPoint or Prezi. As always, **your audience should still determine the method** by which you share these visuals (laptop, tablet, hard copy).

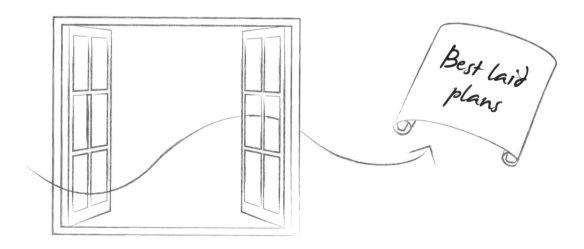

With Just 4 Hours to Go . . .

Let's face it; there's not a huge amount you can do to fix a broken presentation in 4 hours. In fact, the very *worst* thing you can do with such a limited time ahead of you is to attempt to change too much. You must accept the fact: you've got little choice but to make the most out of what you've already got.

Review your presentation and identify the **one key message** you need to share with your audience. Write this down, and refer to it throughout the review of the slides or visuals.

Work your way through the slides/visuals, removing as many words as you feel comfortable. (Hint: Start with the verbs and move on from there!)

Do a slide sense check by reviewing each slide, and ensure that it helps drive your key message. If not, tweak or lose.

If delivered by laptop or tablet, double-check all animations and slide transitions to ensure there are no nasty surprises!

Go through the entire deck of visuals to check no rogue slides have made their way in as a result of copying and pasting from other sources.

And Then . . .

Practice the presentation as much as you can in front of a mirror. Time is short, but this will help you at least ensure you are fully acquainted with each element of the presentation.

With 24 Hours to Go . . .

Although it may not feel like it when you're in the eye of the storm, the good news is that 24 hours leaves you with plenty of time to polish and buff your presentation into something more engaging. Granted, it may not have the firepower of a fully optimized presentation, but it can still deliver on many fronts. It's just a matter of getting your priorities straight.

Message (30%)	Content (40%)	Visuals (30%)
Take time to write down your presentation objectives (Must-Intend-Like). This will refocus your mind and help you identify the content and visuals that are truly engaging your audience and pointing them in the right direction.	Print out all your slides, and lay them on the floor.	Can you easily swap content out for images or diagrams?
With the must-intend-like and key message in mind, take 30 minutes out to create a very high-level story structure to help you engage with the audience.	Now check your existing content against your high-level story structure to determine what needs to stay and what can be discarded. Check that a Call To Action not only exists but also is aligned to your must-intend-like and key message.	Planned carefully, time should allow you to use the likes of PowerPoint's SmartArt function to convert wordy slides into more visual formats.

And Then . . .

Grab a colleague, friend, or spouse and deliver the presentation to that person. After feedback on your style, ask the most important question: **What was the takeaway message** from the presentation?

- If it matches with your original key message, well done.

- If not, review content and visuals again (the extra effort will be worth it).

With One Week to Go . . .

It may not feel like it when you've been given a paltry five working days to prepare for an important presentation, but the reality is that this is plenty of time to make a difference. The nature of Eyeful's business is that we are often called in at the very last minute to make a difference to a presentation. Often, we are able to do it by simply following a structured and sensible approach.

It's all a matter of **using the time wisely** and to maximum impact. Allocating a few hours early on to profile the audience and package your message in as engaging a way as possible is priceless. This way, you'll spend less time worrying about distractions such as templates, fonts, and animations.

40%	25%	35%
Message (Day 1)	**Content (Day 2)**	**Visuals (Days 2–3)**

Based on your knowledge of the audience, pull together a heat map, and then review how best to share your message by developing a storyflow document.

Present the heat map and storyflow document to colleagues. Ask them to challenge and play devil's advocate against your approach. Listen carefully, tweak accordingly, and then preserve this structure in aspic. Don't be tempted to keep going back and changing it; further meddling is unlikely to deliver better results.

In conjunction with your approved presentation structure and message, sift through the content and identify which elements need to remain and which can be left on the cutting room floor.

Draw out your slides on paper, and share them with colleagues in their rawest form. What works? What doesn't? By working on paper, you will be able to acknowledge feedback and make changes easily and quickly.

When comfortable with the flow of the story and happy with the feedback and layout of your visuals, you can start to commit them to PowerPoint/Keynote/Prezi or hard copy.

And Then . . . (Day 4)

- Allocate at least half a day to rehearsing the presentation in front of an audience (ideally colleagues but friends, partners, and pets are also allowed!).

- If possible, video record yourself presenting and then review. At this stage, worry less about the way you are standing or your voice's projection; focus more on the message you are delivering. Make it clear and with a call to action.

Underpinning all of these coping strategies is the simple fact that presentations—and more important, your audiences—deserve a decent investment of time. Last-minute panics over a presentation should be a rare headache rather than a modus operandi. The most engaging and powerful presentations are intelligent, considered, and planned pieces of communication.

The best bit of advice I can offer is this: Do *whatever* is necessary to manage your time accordingly and deliver the presentation your audience and your message deserves.

Conclusion

Element   A B C D E F G **H**

H

THE PRESENTATION LAB

Conclusion

H₁

So there you have it—lessons learned and theories born from almost a decade of working with companies large and small on their presentations, all boiled down into the Presentation Lab formula and method. My hope is that, if nothing else, the thoughts and examples within the book have prompted you to take a moment to rethink your approach to presentations.

Presentations are worth rethinking for the simple reason that when crafted with care and consideration, they have incredible power. Over the years, presentations have been the catalyst for great historic movements, for making positive change and for sharing new ideas. They have been the launch pad for life-changing inventions, for market shifting commercial decisions, and for delivering new and exciting business thinking.

If you take a step back and review the Presentation Lab formula, you'll recognize a few similarities with the approaches taken by the great orators of history. Winston Churchill, Margaret Thatcher, Martin Luther King, and Steve Jobs all understood the power of connecting with an audience. They embraced the beauty of a simple and clear message and delivered it within a story structure that transcended the need for PowerPoint decks or Prezi zoom animations. And ultimately, they changed lives through the power of engaging, audience-focused presentations.

And now it's your turn . . .

Granted, your mission may not be as lofty or grandiose as those aforementioned but I guarantee it's still important. Important enough to employ the Presentation Lab formula and methodology to ensure you get closer to your audience, that your message and content is crystal clear, and that it's supported with visuals that spark a reaction.

And if that's not the case . . . don't bother presenting. You'll be saving yourself and your audience a whole bunch of time.

So in conclusion, be bold, be brave, and recognize that the opportunity to present is a huge privilege afforded you by the audience. Don't waste it (oh, and have fun doing it while you're at it—it shows).

Messages
Ideas

the formula that expands your

WORLD

References

Element   A B C D E F G H

References

Hawking, S. *A Brief History of Time: From Big Bang to Black Holes*. London: Bantam,1995.

Kawasaki, G. *The 10/20/30 Rule of PowerPoint*. Blog. 2005.

Kosslyn, S. M. *Clear and to the Point: Eight Psychological Principles for Compelling PowerPoint® Presentations*. New York: Oxford University Press, 2007.

Kosslyn, S. M., R. A. Kievit, A. G. Russell, and J. M. Shephard. *PowerPoint® Presentation Flaws and Failures: A Psychological Analysis*. Stanford, CA: Center for Advanced Study in the Behavioral Sciences, Stanford University, 2012.

Lester, P. M. "Syntactic Theory of Visual Communication." California State University at Fullerton, 1994–1996.

Moon, Jon. *How To Make an IMPACT: Influence, Inform and Impress with Your Reports, Presentations, Business Documents, Charts and Graphs* (Financial Times Series). London: Financial Times/Prentice Hall, 2007.

Poehm, M. *The PowerPoint Fallacy: Still Presenting or Already Fascinating?* Geneva. Poehm Seminarfactory, 2011.

Reynolds, G. *Presentation Zen: Simple Ideas on Presentation Design and Delivery (Voices That Matter)*. Berkeley: New Riders: 2011.

THE PRESENTATION LAB

Index

Element   A B C D E F G H

THE PRESENTATION LAB

Index

A

Act phase, of Audience Pathway, 78–79
advertising, storytelling and, 43
analogies, use of, 130–137
animated timelines, 196
Apple
    iPad, 184
    Jobs, 76, 88, 89, 190
    Keynote, 190–193
audience
    attention of, 17, 56, 178
    case studies, 212, 217, 223, 229
    combining visual and verbal elements for, 126
    complexity of, 58–73
    connecting with, 36
    developing presentation for, 54
    engagement of, 76, 80–81, 168–170, 176, 200, 242(*See also* presentation tools)
    informative presentations and, 66, 68
    needs of, 6
    Pathway to, 74–81(*See also* Audience Pathway)
    persuasive presentations and, 64, 70
    respect for, 55–57
Audience Pathway, 74–81
    Act phase, 78–79
    Call to Action and, 78
    Engage phase, 76
    Establish phase, 75
    Evaluate phase, 77
    navigating, 80–81
    phases, overview, 74

B

bar charts, 156
bid presentations
    case study, 211–215
    as persuasive, 70
Blended Presenting
    defined, 168–169
    example, 180–183
    for salespeople, 206–207
    wheel for, 185
    See also delivery
brainstorming process, 82–85
business storytelling, 38–47
    importance of communication for, 39–40
    structure of story, 42–46
    themes, 44

C

Call to Action, 78, 93
case studies, 208–233
    bid presentation, 211–215
    conference presentation, 216–221
    internal presentation, 228–233
    sales presentation, 222–227
charts, 156
Churchill, Winston, 76, 118
Cloud-based services, Prezi and, 194
coaching companies, 6
Cognitive Load Theory, 22
color, for charts, 156
Columbia (NASA), 16